Sam Smith has been called many things over the years, among them "an island of reason and information in a sea of narcissistic blather" (Washington's *City Paper*); "one of the few independent voices left" (Eugene McCarthy); "a wonderful combination of being absolutely realistic about the vagaries of people in political life while still being an idealist" (Peter Edelman); "one of a small group of whites with whom many blacks would trust their political lives" (Chuck Stone in the *Washingtonian*); and "a capital curmudgeon" (*Washington Post*) with "a reputation for wit, intelligence, and anger" (*Chicago Tribune*). Claiming the longest running act on the off-Broadway of Washington journalism, for over three decades Sam Smith has edited alternative papers in the capital and won a number of journalism awards (his article on the savings-and-loan bailout was selected as one of the top ten undercovered stories of the past decade by the *Utne Reader*). He has also been a radio newsman and a guest commentator on radio and television. He helped to found the National Drug Strategies Network, the new populist Alliance for Democracy, the DC Statehood

Party, the Association of State Green Parties, the Center for Voting and Democracy, the DC Community Humanities Council, and the Capitol Hill Arts Workshop. He has been a community newspaper editor, president of a home and school association, elected neighborhood commissioner, and helped start a neighborhood crime watch. Smith now edits *The Progressive Review* and recently authored *Shadows of Hope: A Freethinker's Guide to Politics in the Time of Clinton* (Indiana). He lives in Washington, D.C., with his wife, historian Kathryn Schneider Smith.

Kathy Smith

Sam Smith's Great American Political Repair Manual

Sam Smith's Great American Political Repair Manual

HOW TO REBUILD OUR COUNTRY SO THE POLITICS AREN'T BROKEN AND POLITICIANS AREN'T FIXED

W. W. NORTON & COMPANY * NEW YORK * LONDON

This Land Is Your Land
Words and music by Woody Guthrie
TRO © Copyright 1956 (Renewed) 1958 (Renewed) 1970
Ludlow Music, Inc., New York, New York
Used by permission

Thinking about the Longstanding Problems of Virtue and Happiness
By Tony Kushner
© Copyright 1995, Tony Kushner
Theater Communications Group, New York

They Thought They Were Free
By Milton Mayer
© Copyright 1955. All rights reserved.
University of Chicago Press

For information about permission to reproduce selections from this book, write to Permissions, W. W. Norton & Company, Inc., 500 Fifth Avenue, New York, NY 10010.

The text of this book is composed in Sabon and Citizen, with the display set in Bauhaus.
Composition by ComCom, an RR Donnelley & Sons Company.
Manufacturing by Haddon Craftsmen Bloomsburg Division of RR Donnelley & Sons.

Library of Congress Cataloging-in-Publication Data
Smith, Sam, 1937–
 [Great American political repair manual]
 Sam Smith's great American political repair manual : how to rebuild our country so the politics aren't broken and politicians aren't fixed.
  p. cm.
 Includes bibliographical references.
 ISBN 0-393-04122-0. — ISBN 0-393-31627-0 (pbk).
 1. Political participation—United States. 2. United States—Politics and government—1993– I. Title.
JK1764.S555 1997
323'.042'0973—dc21
                                                                        97-18636
                                                                        CIP

W. W. Norton & Company, Inc., 500 Fifth Avenue, New York, N.Y. 10110
http://www.wwnorton.com

W. W. Norton & Company Ltd., 10 Coptic Street, London WC1A 1PU

1 2 3 4 5 6 7 8 9 0

This book is dedicated
to a great American:
YOU

Our leading men are not of much account and
never have been, but the average of the people is
immense, beyond all history. . . . We will not have
great individuals or great leaders, but a great
average bulk, unprecedentedly great.

—Walt Whitman

How . . .

**As well as useful charts, hints, caveats, lists, addresses,
stats, Web sites, and pithy quotes too numerous to mention**

Sam Smith's Great American Political Repair Manual

1. How to read this book

Construct your own interactive medium

Warning

This book is not harmful to pregnant women, small children, or persons on medication. It may, however, cause temporary dyspepsia and other distress to those unaccustomed to more than casual reflection on political matters. To alleviate these symptoms, observe the procedures below.

My friend Larry, the banker, knows how to read a book. Open up one of his books, and you'll find the margins sprinkled

> We read to know we're not alone.
> —Student in the movie
> *Shadowlands*

with comments in green ink—sometimes thoughtful, sometimes irate, sometimes even obscene. You see, Larry doesn't just read a book; he converses with it, he argues with it, sometimes he even yells at it.

> Writing . . . but a different name for conversation.
> —Laurence Sterne

My friend Teresa, the longtime community activist, knows how to watch TV. I ran into her awhile back, and she told me that she had been following a local talk show on which I regularly appeared. "How'm I doing?" I asked.

"Oh, you're doing okay, Sam," she replied. "Sometimes I want to throw that TV right back at you, but most of the time you do pretty good."

In an age when the media teach us that life is a vicarious experience, Larry and Teresa have refused to become passive consumers of information. They know that a book or a TV show is only a part of the story and that the most important part is in our own minds and hearts as we read or watch.

I hope you'll read this book in the same way. I've done my part, and now you've got to do yours. Think about it. React to it. Talk to someone else about it (or get together with others and talk to a lot of somebody elses about it). Contact the organizations and read the books listed in the back. Organize around something you find here. Change your mind about something because of it.

You can also scribble furiously in the margins or throw the book at the TV if it makes you feel better. After all, books are an interactive medium too.

> If you'd like, you can send your thoughts to me c/o W. W. Norton, 500 Fifth Avenue, New York, NY 10110. Or you can e-mail me at ssmith@iqc.org or visit the *American Repair Manual* home page at:
>
> http://emporium.turnpike.net/P/ProRev/repair.htm
>
> There you'll find updated lists of organizations working on some of the things discussed in this book, other good projects and new ideas, as well as comments from readers and the author.

Disclaimer

In this book you may find what seem to be extremely novel ideas. In fact, most of them have been around for a while, and some have been around for centuries. You just haven't seen them discussed in your daily paper or on *Nightline*.

When confronted with a new idea, many of the media and many of our leaders tend to dismiss it as "untested," "radical," "off the wall," or "dangerous." So, as you read this book, keep in mind the following:

- Neither the author nor anything in this book has been responsible for the current strains in the American economy, the degradation of the environment, the deep alienation of large numbers of our citizens, or the quality of TV shows. All these phenomena are products of an American establishment that tends to dismiss new ideas as untested, radical, off the wall, or dangerous.
- The author does not guarantee that every idea in this book will work. Some may even prove politically or technically impractical. He does, however, guarantee that a country repaired along the lines suggested here will be a far healthier, happier, more productive and decent America than the one we live in today.

2. How to listen to America unplugged
What are we trying to fix anyway?

Before we start trying to fix the something we call America, we'd better remind ourselves of what America is. Thanks to all the

> Can do.
>
> —Motto of the U.S. Navy Seabees

commercial, political, and romantic symbolism surrounding the word, it is not an easy task.

It's also not easy when so many find the symbolism false and the reality cruel. You don't feel like singing when you're searching for a life jacket.

Yet even for many disillusioned or skeptical Americans there remains just below the surface the idea of a place worth saving. To find this America buried in our hearts, we have to turn off the amps of propaganda and hype, the reverb and distortion of our fears and failures, and listen to the country unplugged. Some of the best things can be heard only when everything else is still.

There are lots of different ways to think about America. Some people like to call America a nation of laws, but that sounds as if we just spend our days obeying regulations—the sort of place only an attorney could love.

Other people think of America as a government or as a geographical subdivision; that is fair enough, but it fails to give the real flavor of the place or explain the strong feelings many Americans have for their land. Many people think of America as stretching from the Arctic to Tierra del

Fuego, and that's right too, but in this book we use the word much as people in the Big Apple refer to their hometown as New York, even though the residents of Buffalo think of New York as reaching from Canada to the Hudson.

Here are three things that come to mind when I think of America:

An environment

An environment is more than a place; it is a condition, it is sustenance, it is shelter, it is a thousand invisible threads tying us to that which lies way out there.

The natural habitat of America long overwhelmed anything that

> Fix it up,
> Make it do,
> Wear it out,
> Use it up,
> Do without.
> —Maine saying

could be built by mere humans, a fact that shaped our character and our culture. It has, to be sure, created oddities: We have become the most ecologically wasteful of nations yet have given the world some of its finest environmental writings. We have preserved some of the world's great natural spaces, but only after virtually exterminating those who lived there. The grandeur of our land has at times made us profligate, at other times humble and religious. We are deeply romantic about the wilderness yet have been ruthless in its exploitation.

In the past one hundred years or so we have learned how to replace nature with systems, technology, machines, and institutions. For a long time it seemed to work. It appeared that America had a lifetime pass to progress, that Americans could do even better than nature.

> This land is your land, this land
>   is my land
> From California to the New York
>   island
> From the redwood forest to the
>   Gulf Stream waters
> This land was made for you and
>   me
>   —Woody Guthrie
>   ©

But a few decades ago things started to go awry. Our cities began to disintegrate. Families broke up with startling frequency. Real income slid, and jobs drifted overseas. The environment became less a cornucopia and more a problem. Our nonnatural systems no longer seemed as wonderful as they once had.

> **FOUR LAWS OF ECOLOGY**
>
> 1. Everything is connected to everything else.
> 2. Everything must go somewhere.
> 3. Nature knows best.
> 4. There is no such thing as a free lunch.
>
> —Barry Commoner

As these artificial systems failed us, some Americans began returning to natural ones, finding in them a wisdom and sustenance the constructed systems could not provide. Farmers rediscovered nonchemical ways to protect their crops. Communities and businesses began to recycle and seek self-sufficiency. Individuals began downshifting their consumption and lifestyles. And planners discovered long-ignored benefits in treading more softly on the earth.

Even after generations of frequent and massive mistreatment the American environment is still vital enough to welcome us back, asking only that this time we play by its rules. Its message is simple: that we do not have to belong to artificial systems; we can belong to the land itself.

A people

We can also define ourselves as a people. Because of the variety of our backgrounds, it is not, however, a primeval past or cultural similarity but rather a shared present and future that bind us.

Sometimes—such as in times of massive disaster—we act on this communality. We suddenly and without instruction mobilize ourselves to help those miles away, recognizing for a few days or a few months that *they* are also one of us. We do the same thing when we're having fun; at a concert or a festival we feel a bond with everyone sharing the same experience. And when an admired leader dies, we grieve together.

As with the environment, though, we are inconsistent. America remains one of the most favored destinations for those seeking freedom and a better life, yet the newcomer often finds hostility as well as freedom, discrimination as well as opportunity.

In the end it is not the culture from which we came but the one each of us is helping to create that will matter. It is our common fate

> You can not spill a drop of American blood without spilling the blood of the whole world.
>
> —Herman Melville

rather than our disparate pasts that will ultimately describe, redeem, or destroy us.

Ideals

What we take for granted—that a nation and a people should be organized around a set of principles—was once considered revolutionary and even today remains remarkable. It also takes a lot of work and a lot of argument. But it is one of the things that best defines America.

As with our personal ideals, our country has repeatedly failed to live up to what it proclaims. But while we may not always practice what we preach, at least we do not preach what we practice. The mere existence of our principles and the willingness of large numbers of Americans to work for them gives the country a special character.

> You have just taken an oath of allegiance to the United States. Of allegiance to whom? Of allegiance to no one, unless it be God. Certainly not of allegiance to those who temporarily represent this great government. You have taken an oath of allegiance to a great ideal, to a great body of principles, to a great hope of the human race.
> —Woodrow Wilson, speaking to a group of newly naturalized citizens

In short, America is not the answer; it is only a good place to look for the answer. America has never been perfect; it's just been a place where it was easier to fix things that were broken.

The ability to repair ourselves has long been one of our great characteristics as a people and a nation. This book is written in the faith that we still possess it.

BASEBALL

Baseball is among the most democratic of sports. Each player is given great freedom and specific turf to guard, but this individuality works only when all the members of a team cooperate. Baseball, Eugene McCarthy has pointed out, is unique in that the game is not restricted by either time or space; games theoretically can go on forever, as can an out-of-the-park homer. He also notes that while in other sports you might hear fan suggestions that the ref be fired, it is during baseball games that the crowds cry, "Kill the ump!" Thus the game, like America itself, celebrates not only a deep distrust of authority and a lack of limits but also cooperation, individuality, and community.

TWO AMERICAN METAPHORS . . .

JAZZ

The essence of jazz is the same as that of democracy: the greatest amount of individual freedom consistent with a healthy community. Each musician is allowed extraordinary liberty during a solo and then is expected conscientiously to back up the other musicians in turn. The two most exciting moments in jazz are during flights of individual virtuosity and when the entire musical group seems to become one. The genius of jazz (and democracy) is that the same people are willing and able to do both.

Here's how Wynton Marsalis describes it: "Jazz is a music of conversation, and that's what you need in a democracy. You have to be willing to hear another person's point of view and respond to it. . . . The principle of American democracy is that you have freedom; the question is: How will you use it? Which is also the central question in jazz."

An American Parts List

250 million Americans

190 million motor vehicles

37 billion hours spent each year waiting for something

361,000 churches, synagogues, and mosques

36 million elementary school kids

37 million citizens in poverty

3. How NOT to repair the country
Ten ways we really screw things up

Consider this:

- Only 34 percent of eligible Americans voted in the 1994 congressional election. During the same period voter turnout for European parliamentary elections ranged from 77 percent in Greece to 89 percent in Italy.
- When this book was written, only 2 percent of us thought the country was in excellent shape, two thirds said it was in only fair or poor shape.
- Less than a third of us thought the country was going in the right direction.
- Thirty-nine percent agreed that the federal government had become "so large and powerful that it poses an immediate threat to the rights and freedoms of ordinary citizens." When Gallup dropped the word *immediate*, those agreeing rose to 52 percent.
- In 1964, 79 percent of Americans said they trusted the government in Washington to do what was right. By 1994 that figure had dropped to 22 percent.
- Only 58 percent of Americans thought that the country would even exist as one nation a hundred years from now.
- In another poll 18 percent went so far as to believe they must arm themselves against the government.*

*Here and elsewhere in this book (and in real life for that matter) polls should be considered only as circumstantial evidence. On the other hand, Thoreau pointed out that some circumstantial evidence is pretty strong—as when you find a trout in your milk. That's a good clue someone has been watering the milk.

Now, according to what we were taught in school, there should be enough Americans who are unhappy to come together and change things. But there are some problems with this theory. For example, the folks who don't want things to change have hired tens of thousands of people in Washington and in your state capital just to make sure that they, and not you, get their way. When a bill comes before Congress or the state legislature, they are there. You aren't.

But there's another important factor: the way we go about attempting to solve our problems. Before looking at some things that might work, let's consider some things that haven't and won't—no matter how hard we try.

1. Mistaking the "system" for America

The "system" is not America. The "system" is not us. It represents neither the land nor its people, neither our ideals nor our souls. One reason so many of us feel disaffected is that we know in our hearts—even if we can't think of the right words or actions—that much of what we find in the "system" no longer matches what we believe America should be about. Yet the "system" runs America.

Some have reacted to this with anger, some with paranoia, many more with apathy. Most of us continue to muddle along with little idea of what to do except to scream at someone or try to forget about it all.

Yet if this is all we do, we remain a functioning cog in the very system that troubles us so much. We remain its silent consumers, its faithful constituents, and its full-time staff.

2. Trying to "fix" the system

This book is not about fixing the system. The system is working fine. It has in fact spread like kudzu to every corner of American life; it

> Our goal is not to overthrow the system but to make it irrelevant.
> —1960s saying

hangs on our souls and suffocates the branches of our communities. It increasingly consumes our time, noses into our affairs, pollutes our air and our airwaves, tells us what we can and cannot do, reduces us to a number, defaces our culture with commercial graffiti, and sponges up for itself every drop of wealth it can find.

Instead this book is about transforming and replacing the system—and the subsystems—that control America. It is about repairing our own culture, our own politics, our spirit, our ideals, and our faith in ourselves, so we no longer come to the system as its tools, as "human resources," "stakeholders," or "consumers"* but rather as citizens and owners. So the system serves and does not rule.

But the "system" isn't going to tell us how to replace or transform itself. Its politicians, in the employ of major donors, will not show us how. Nor will the handful of media conglomerates that control most of what we read, see, and hear. Nor global corporations with their declining allegiance to the welfare of a nation they use increasingly primarily as a mail drop. We're on our own.

3. Thinking you can't beat city hall

Here's another way we screw things up. Look at the chart opposite. It illustrates a couple of important points. First, it reminds us that history ain't *Sesame Street*. History is often messy, contradictory, and cruel. It can read like a poorly written first novel. It often doesn't break our way.

On the other hand, the chart also reminds us that we belong to a long tradition of redefinition, revival, rebellion, and rediscovery that has kept this country from going to seed or to tyranny. It has been the repeated dissatisfaction—even shame and disgust—that Americans have felt about their own country, followed by the application of practical remedies, that has saved us again and again.

We are now in one of those periods in which everything seems weighted against the interests of the ordinary human being. We basically have two choices. One is to do nothing and just let it get worse. The other is to follow in the footsteps of those before us who refused to let this happen—those who refused to believe they couldn't beat city hall.

A good way to think about the history of our country is that it has in-

*Through such words the system regularly diminishes the role of the citizen. Consider, for example, what a *stakeholder* really is: someone with temporary custody of property in dispute between two or more parties to which the stakeholder has no claim. In other words, a bystander who gets no benefit out of the situation, no matter who wins.

Bucking the system: A scorecard

Periods	People win	System wins
Late 18th century	• End of monarchy & nobility • End of British colonial rule • Creation of a constitutional democracy	• Eradication of Indian peoples (continues into 20th century)
Early 19th century	• End of property requirements for voting	• Strengthening of the slave system
Mid-19th century	• End of slavery • Union organizing • End of women being considered husbands' legal property	• Harsh factory conditions • Anti-labor court rulings • Strikebreaking by police and troops
Late 19th century	• Black progress during Reconstruction era • Populist movement • Urban power for new ethnic groups	• Small-scale economic democracy largely replaced by the modern corporation • Rampant corruption of government by corporate interests and urban ethnic machines • End of Reconstruction era, rise of segregation as a legal concept • Supreme Court's giving the rights of living persons to corporations
Early 20th century	• Women's suffrage • Large-scale labor organizing • The New Deal & social welfare programs • Antitrust activity	• Period of corporate excess
Late 20th century	• Civil rights movement • Women's movement • Consumer movement • Environmental movement • The 18-year-old vote • Gay rights movement	• Rise of the military-industrial complex • Trickle-down economics • Corporate and bank deregulation • Declining real wages • Flight of business abroad • Paramilitary occupation of urban areas • Rise of corporate health care systems • Massive corruption of politics and government • Retreat from civil rights

volved repeated conflict between the soul and institutions—between people and places on the one hand and a succession of systems desiring to exploit, subjugate, or supplant them on the other.

You can say that one of the great characteristics of Americans has been not merely opposition to a system of the moment but antipathy toward unnatural systems in general—opposition to all systems that revoke, replace, or restrain the intrinsic rights of human beings.

4. Thinking the answer is more rules

The number of new laws and regulations created by federal, state, and local government has leaped in recent decades. Some of these laws have been needed. Some have been attempts to patch up laws we thought were needed but never worked quite right. Do this enough times—as we have with health care—and you can end up with a patchwork policy that *nobody* ever asked for.

More than a few of the laws—especially in times of budget cutbacks when positive new programs don't stand a chance—are just designed to convince voters that their legislators are actually doing something. If you listen carefully, you may even hear these politicians rooting around in the evening news and morning papers for something more to prohibit or regulate.

Laws should be handled like prescription drugs, but many of our politicians think of them as being more like popcorn or M&M's—something to munch on. This is unfortunate since much of America's success to date can be traced to one simple rule: Don't make too many rules. Much of America's failure to date has come from ignoring this rule.

> There ain't no rules around here. We're trying to accomplish something.
>
> —Thomas Edison

5. Misplacing the center

Another way we fail to repair things is by thinking the answers will be found in the middle of the road. For many people the American political center sits halfway between the current Democratic and Republican parties. That's neat and orderly, but it just isn't accurate. History shows, for example, that on domestic social issues *every* president—Republican or Democrat, from

Roosevelt to Carter (including Nixon and Ford)—was substantially to the left of Reagan, Bush, and Clinton. On issues such as welfare or civil liberties, Clinton even turned to the right of Reagan and Bush.

In fact, both parties have drifted so far to the right over the past two decades that if they were playing in the NFL, the ball would have to be hiked from the press box.

Even talking about left and right or liberal and conservative doesn't explain that much. For example, supporters of decentralized government include both conservatives and progressives. Similarly, both Democrats and Republicans have helped build the massive federal government.

Or: how much power should government have to carry out its policies? To interfere with our personal lives? On some of these issues, there were conservatives who proved more "liberal" (in the traditional sense) than the Clinton White House.

> There's nothing in the middle of the road but a yellow stripe and a lot of dead armadillos.
> —Jim Hightower

Or: what about conservatives who are all for the freedom to bear arms yet are willing to restrict freedom of speech and religion? Or: libertarians and greens believe in considerable personal freedom but disagree on property rights.

And where do we place the Perot supporter who agrees with the Republicans on the budget but opposes both the GOP and the Democrats on NAFTA?

If you ask important people in politics, think tanks, or the media where they stand politically, many will say "in the center." A lot of these folks like the

---

CENTERSPEAK

Centrists speak their own language, which has been called Otoh-Botoh (for "on the one hand . . . , but on the other hand . . ."). If you read or listen to Otoh-Botoh for too long, you may get a bad case of mego (for "mine eyes glaze over"). In the nineteenth century people who talked Otoh-Botoh were called mugwumps—because they sat on a fence with their mugs on one side and their wumps on the other.

> What used to be called liberal is now called radical;
> What used to be called radical is now called insane.
> What used to be called reactionary is now called moderate,
> and what used to be called insane is now called solid conservative thinking.
> —Tony Kushner

center because it makes them sound reasonable and moderate. It also allows them to call other people extremists or gadflies or wishful thinkers for disagreeing with the conventional wisdom of the moment. Some members of the American elite have made whole careers of being measured and cautious. They like to write somber columns asking pompous questions like "Can the Center Hold?" What they really mean is: Can they hold on to their power? Ironically, polls suggest that the American people don't view this elite as in the center at all—rather it is neither trusted nor admired.

Even if you do find the center, it's not necessarily the best place to be. My navigation instructor at Coast Guard Officer Candidate School explained it well: "If you take a navigational fix and it places you on one side of a rock and then you take another fix and it places you on the other side of the rock, don't split the difference." Unfortunately it's a rule not often followed in American politics.

We have to move toward a politics that offers a choice not between left and right but between corporatism and democracy, not between big government and big business but between overbearing institutions and supportive communities, and not between oppression and anarchy but between the force of the state and the good sense of its citizens. We need a new politics that offers not only new policies but a new way of going about politics, one that is centered on consent rather than on power. This is the sort of politics that we'll be talking about in this book.

6. Blaming the wrong thing

Mistake No. 6 is a bad one. When times are tough, people start looking for someone to blame. From ancient days on, people have tried to feel better by feeding someone else to the lions. Politicians and the media are often glad to help.

Here are some of the people currently being blamed for America's troubles: illegal immigrants, blacks, feminists, welfare mothers, Arabs, gays, militia members, and skinheads.

Now in fact, no woman—feminazi or otherwise—has an opinion show with anywhere close to the audience of that of Rush Limbaugh. Rush nonetheless would have you believe that he and his conservative friends are just barely repelling the femalian hordes.

Similarly there is no bank or other financial institution that is run by an illegal immigrant, and there is only one black in the U.S. Senate. (In fact, in all our history only ninety-five blacks have been elected to Congress.) The major job loss in America is not due to Latinos coming into the country but to business being sent out of the country by some very Anglo chief executives.

Here's how to do a little reality check:

- What are the ethnic character and sex of those with whom you work?
- Now break it down. What about people who earn less than yourself? People who earn the same? Those above you? The boss?
- What about your local council? The mayor? Your minister or rabbi?
- Now what about the sanitation workers? The bus drivers? The janitors?
- How about the people on the Sunday TV talk shows? Any signs of Arabs or skinheads taking over *The McLaughlin Group?*
- Who lives in the best part of your town?
- How many women or Latinos are running the biggest businesses where you live?

ELUSIVE STEREOTYPE #127

When the Oklahoma City bombing occurred, papers such as the *New York Times* and the *Washington Post,* columnists such as Mike Royko, and at least three of the major networks rushed to speculate that the attack was the work of Arab terrorists. Royko even suggested bombing an Arab country in retaliation. When it turned out the suspects came from the Midwest rather than from the Mideast, another columnist, Richard Roeper, asked, "Does that mean we conduct overnight bombings of Arizona and Kansas and Michigan now?"

The point is simply this: What we think we know and what really is can be quite different. A public school teacher in Washington, D.C., drew ten stick figures on the blackboard. She asked her all-black class to assume that these figures represented the population of the United States. The question: How many of the stick figures should be black? The typical response was nine. The kids had seen no farther than their own neighborhood.

While the reach of modern media should make us all more cosmopolitan, it often doesn't work like that. This is in part because of what we choose to watch and in part because what is chosen for us to see. TV's typical view of the outside world is of a place rife with danger. Talk shows and programs like *Cops* can make it feel as if you're under siege. CNN constantly scans the world for new battlegrounds.

Before television you got most of the bad news from your own town and neighborhood. Now you can get bad news from any part of the globe, any time of day or night. It's hard not to worry.

The media also like quick explanations for their stories. A multiple murder by a sniper occurs, and within hours a motivation has been assigned—the accused is a black nationalist, a neo-Nazi, a disgruntled postal worker, a radical environmentalist—and so one more stereotype becomes a little more fixed in our consciousness. Complex explanations come later, if at all. Meanwhile, the headline reads LONER

KILLS TEN. And every shy person in America takes another lump.

Politicians—especially during election season—often try to play on the fears such stories create. And it's bipartisan: The Al Gore presidential campaign used the Willie Horton gambit against Dukakis even before Bush; it just didn't catch on.

Making some people afraid of other people is one of the best ways to control *all* of them. In the days before the civil rights movement, southern politics was based in no small part on keeping poor whites afraid of poor blacks. During the McCarthy era the public was taught to be terrified of Communists—although later it turned out that among the major sources of party members were FBI agents and informants. Since the end of the Cold War the "Arab terrorist" has become a favorite political goblin, along with various evil characters lurking on the Internet—including a horrible new specter identified by the FBI as "file-encrypting child pornographers."

Which is not to say that there aren't sex fiends, terrorists, and brutal murderers about, some of whom may be computer geeks, Arabs, or skinheads. Or that there are not clandestine groups with evil intent willing and able to blow up a building or a plane. The problem comes when marginal violence is magnified into a national trend. Or when adjectives become not descriptions of specifics but generic characterizations. Scientists warn against the latter by saying that correlation does not necessarily prove causation. In other words, just because the mess on the carpet and your television set are in the same room doesn't mean that the TV pooped on your rug. It might have been your dog, who is, at the moment, nowhere to be found.

One way to keep things in perspective is to count the bodies. It's hard to get good data on domestic terrorism, but we do know that only 171 people were indicted in the United States during the 1980s in the broad category of "terrorism and related activities." According to the State Department, in the six years prior to 1995 there were only 9 international terrorist incidents in all of North America, compared to 821 in Latin America. Between 1989 and 1995 there were fewer bombing deaths nationwide than people murdered in New York City in a single year (the bombings included everything from Mafia retribution, insurance cover-ups, angry spouses, and apolitical acts of madness to Oklahoma City and right-wing sabotage such as that directed against abortion clinics). Not even the FBI seemed that concerned about domestic terrorism. In the decade prior to 1996 only 19 of its 9,553 applications for wiretapping permission involved arson, bombing, or firearms. The Unabomber has been less deadly than a moderately vengeful urban gang. And so forth.

Now let's count some other bodies. Such as the 60,000 Americans killed in Vietnam. Or nearly that many casualties in the war on drugs, which has left in its wake a greater death rate among young urban black males than there was among black GIs in Vietnam.

Or the nearly 2 million Vietnamese killed during our war there, most by air attacks that dropped twice as many bombs as we did in all of World War II—nearly one 500-pound bomb per person. Or the 1 million civilians our strategic bombing killed in Japan before we even got to Hiroshima and Nagasaki. Or the more than 2 million civilians we killed in our bombing runs over North Korea. Or the half million children who died in Iraq during the first years of the post–Gulf War embargo.

Trace this extraordinary violence to the source, and you come not upon America's political extremes but to the heart of its establishment. Even the KKK, so often cited as an example of the ever-present danger from extremism, was in fact powerful not because it was extreme but because it was at the precise center of so much of America—holding political, judicial, and law enforcement offices as well as hiding beneath its robes. In some towns lynching parties were even announced in the local paper.

As the Andrews Sisters used to sing, "Don't worry 'bout strangers; keep your eye on your best friend."

7. Doing the same thing—only harder

This is one of the most common mistakes in politics. It's what kept us bogged down in Vietnam so long. It's what keeping us mired in the war on drugs. Someone once defined insanity as doing the same thing over and over again and expecting a different result. Many politicians go even further. If it's a war, they escalate; it if it is a program; they increase its budget; if it's a law, they make it tougher. Then everyone wonders why nothing has changed.

> I can't understand why people are frightened of new ideas. I'm frightened of the old ones.
> —Composer John Cage

In fact, a lot of problems just can't be solved without being looked at in a completely new way. Edward de Bono calls this *lateral thinking*.

In vertical thinking, he says, the mind moves "from one solid step to another solid step," not unlike a computer or a legal brief. This sort of thinking is useful and necessary in our daily lives. But it simply will not produce many of the solutions we're seeking. In order to find these, we must make a huge leap, starting not with our previous steps but with the conclusion we desire. As De Bono explains it, "Instead of proceeding step by step in the usual vertical manner, you take up a new and quite arbitrary position. You then work backwards and try to construct a logical path between this new position and the starting point. Should a path prove possible, it must eventually be tested with the full rigors of logic. . . . Even if the arbitrary position does not prove tenable, you may still have generated useful new ideas in trying to justify it."

Here's an example:

HOW TO AVOID BLAMING THE WRONG THING

1. Count the bodies. If something bad is happening, there should be evidence of it. Besides, counting the bodies helps order priorities.
2. Get facts before you get scared. Just because a politician or a journalist says there's a threat doesn't mean there actually is one.
3. Just because it's on TV doesn't mean it's happening to you or your neighborhood. Just because it's at the top of the news doesn't mean it should be at the top of your mind.
4. Fight issues, not people. Your gun-loving, antiabortion neighbor may also oppose plans to store nuclear waste nearby. Find out. After all, most of us are right only part of the time.
5. Don't try to crush those with whom you disagree; convert them.
6. Before "they" can do you any real harm, "they" probably need money and power. If "they" don't have it, you are probably worrying about the wrong "they."

Look at the three sticks.

Now arrange these three sticks in such a way as to form the number nine, without breaking or bending any of the sticks. The problem is impossible to solve using normal logic and vertical thinking. But what if we throw away some of our assumptions and ask weird questions, such as: Which numbering system are we talking about anyway? Or what if we—in a manner that a computer or economist might not condone—just start to play randomly and erratically with the sticks? By either method we might stumble upon the correct answer even though our route to it was slovenly and illogical. Then we might arrange the sticks so:

A fascinating thing about lateral thinking is that once you come upon the solution, it seems so obvious. Not unlike Schopenhauer's three stages of a new idea: In the first stage it is ridiculed. In the second stage it is violently opposed. In the third stage it is considered self-evident.

How does this apply to politics? Here's an example:

Many communities have become concerned over teens' skateboarding and Rollerblading in places where they might endanger others or themselves. These communities, engaging in vertical thinking, pass ordinances that ban such practices in these places. Soon there are few spots in town where skateboarding or Rollerblading is both legal and

> Want to learn how to think laterally? Listen to good comedians. They're always setting up a conclusion and imagining the consequences that might flow from it. For example, comic Steven Wright says he once went fishing with Salvador Dali. Dali was using a dotted line. So he only caught every other fish.

fun. The teens have one more reason to feel alienated from the adults of the community. Some may express this by getting into trouble in some other way.

Peter Capozza, a former Outward Bound instructor who lives in a small town in Maine, saw this problem and applied some lateral thinking to it. He thought first of the desired solution: a place where teens could have fun and where adults wouldn't be annoyed or hit by fun-loving, self-propelled teens.

PETER CAPOZZA'S THREE RULES OF SOCIAL ACTION

1. Try something.
2. If it works, great.
3. If it doesn't, try something else.

He then worked backward. He asked the teens hanging out on the library steps what he would need to provide in order to attract them to a such a place. He got ideas from skateboarders and Rollerbladers, along with sketches and models of ramps that he later helped them construct. He then approached the town council and businesses for a small amount of money to set up ramps, cones, and half pipes in the high school parking lot and to offer basketball and volleyball inside. Not only did it turn out to be a huge success, but the police chief reported a significant drop in teenage incidents over the course of the summer. The one problem was getting the teens to leave at midnight.

8. Being afraid of mistakes

In this book you'll find lots of lateral thinking. Some of it you'll agree with, and some you won't. You will also find mistakes. And ideas that may not pan out. I'm not worried about that, and you shouldn't be either. Being afraid to make mistakes is one of the reasons we find ourselves unable to repair our country.

De Bono notes, "Lateral thinking means getting down into the mud and searching around until a natural causeway is found. The need to be right at every stage and all the time is probably the biggest bar there is to new ideas." In other words, progress needs trial and error; it needs research and development.

One reason there is so little R&D in politics is that politicians are afraid of going out on a limb. Even when research has been done, politicians and the press often just ignore it. As a school board member told me once, "Everyone wants to examine the schools that fail; nobody looks at the ones that work." We have become so habituated to thinking that urban public schools don't work that any suggestion to the contrary seems a bit wacky.

Inventors are different. They know they have to try lots of things before they come across something that will work. Sometimes the solution is even found before the problem, as when a unique sticky substance was created that no one at the company knew quite knew how to use. The ultimate result: Post-It notes. Sometimes the solution is created before the inventor knows how it works. Marconi, for example, believed that if he designed a strong enough transmitter and receiver, he would be able to send messages across the Atlantic Ocean. The

> Albert Camus once explained why he was not willing to die for his beliefs: "What if I'm wrong?"

experts told him he was wrong: The earth was curved, and so the straight-line radio waves would just wander off into space. But the plan worked, and only later did scientists and Marconi discover how radio waves bounced off the ionosphere.

One advantage to not being afraid of failure is that you prepare for it. Being ready for things to go wrong is one of the hallmarks of self-sufficiency. For example, much of the skill of a farmer or a sailor consists of being able to handle problems. The farmer does not say—as a politician or large bureaucracy might—"I will not mow this field because it could break my mower or baler." He buys a welding machine and learns how to repair his own equipment. Similarly the term *damage control*, in its original meaning, had nothing to do with putting out news releases to make everything seem all right but described the elaborate and essential art of saving a ship from disaster.

> An American editor worries his hair gray to see that no typographical mistakes appear on the pages of his magazine. The Chinese editor is wiser than that. He wants to leave his readers the supreme satisfaction of discovering a few typographical mistakes for themselves
>
> —Lin Yutang, a Chinese writer in the 1930s

> How do I work? I grope.
>
> —Albert Einstein

While inventors, artists, and other lateral thinkers are not afraid of mistakes, big institutions and systems are. So afraid of error do these systems become that they spend a phenomenal amount of time and money on standardizing their work and products, controlling the behavior of employees, and creating excuses when things go wrong. By obsessively avoiding the chance of failure, however, these institutions simultaneously stifle genius and make creativity next to impossible.

John McKnight, in *The Careless Society*, argues that here is one of the big differences between institutions and communities. Communities compensate for, and absorb, failure—as when neighbors help out friends or relatives in trouble—while institutions attempt to eradicate it.

9. Letting the mob in

There is a world of difference, however, between simple human error and premeditated malevolence. One of the most remarkable things about American politics over the past thirty years is how often the latter has intruded on the normal workings of our democracy. Many of these incidents have been poorly reported or only briefly covered and then forgotten. The cumulative story has been almost totally ignored.

We need not finally determine who killed JFK and for what reasons to recognize a more generic fact: Our politics has been repeatedly interrupted and distorted by assassins, mobs, rogue intelligence agents and agencies, freelance conspirators, drug runners, massive corruption, illegal financial manipulation, and off-the-shelf government operations. The table on the next page lists a few of the most prominent examples.

These incidents are both a cause and a reflection of the deterioration of American democracy. Transforming our politics calls for neither paranoia nor fatalism on this score, but it does require inoculating the body politic against such occurrences. Much of what is discussed in this book will, as a side benefit, make us less susceptible to mob politics.

10. Trusting *their* experts

A final obstacle to reviving our country is the massive power of the professional elite. When we speak of Washington lobbyists, for example, we are talking primarily about people who represent various professional and corporate interests, ranging from lawyers and doctors to commercial trade associations and individual corporations. Even when lobbies are supposed to be representing ordinary people, they often succumb to overprofessionalization, becoming codependent with the very interests they are supposed to be fighting. Corporate reformer Richard Grossman explains how this has happened in environmental law: "Environmental attorneys have been funneling people's time, energy and resources into a regulatory and administrative law system where even if we 'win' we don't win much; and where there are few mechanisms for shifting rights and powers away from the corporations and towards people, communities and nature."

And what have we gotten from these professional environmentalists? "Laws which legalized the poisoning of air and water, which legalized clear cutting, which left unchallenged the privileges and immunities which corporations had usurped during the past century, and which concentrated power in the hands of appointed regulators and administrators insulated from our reach."

Mob politics: three decades of political racketeering

Administration	Notes
John F. Kennedy • The 1960 election • Castro assassination attempt • The Bay of Pigs • JFK assassination	A mob payoff may have helped rig the crucial Illinois election results. The Kennedy administration approached mobsters for help in an unconsummated assassination attempt against Castro. The Bay of Pigs was an off-the-shelf and off-the-wall idea of CIA adventurists aided by right-wing Cubans. Major questions remain concerning the JFK assassination.
Lyndon B. Johnson • M. L. King assassination • RFK assassination • SE Asian heroin trade	Many investigators are still dissatisfied with official conclusions concerning the King and RFK assassinations. During the LBJ administration the CIA allowed the SE Asian heroin trade to flourish in return for the loyalty of tribes involved—a sort of hook-an-American-for-peace policy.
Richard Nixon • CHAOS • Cambodia • Chile • Watergate	CHAOS was a massive covert program of spying on, and disruption of, progressive groups. Nixon conducted a secret illegal war in Cambodia and planned the demise of democracy in Chile along with the assassination of its president. Watergate was the biggest presidential scandal yet in American history.
Gerald Ford	A quiet period.
Jimmy Carter • October surprise • Debategate	Carter was a target of covert activities. Congressional findings notwithstanding, Russian intelligence files and other foreign sources support the notion that the Reagan campaign made a secret deal with the Iranians to hold the American hostages until after the 1980 election. During the same campaign Carter's debate briefing books were stolen and turned over to the GOP. Carter may have unwittingly contributed to future illicit activity by ordering major layoffs at the CIA. These forced out hundreds of agents, some of whom began free-lancing and later became involved in Iran-contra.
Ronald Reagan • Wall street scandals • S&L scandal • BCCI scandal • Iran-contra	Laissez-faire economics and lack of enforcement encouraged two of the biggest financial scandals in American history. The S&L and BCCI scandals had deep and high-level bipartisan involvement. Reagan pressed a secret and illegal war against Nicaragua. Two-way trade developed with arms going south to

- Latin American drug trade
- Domestic spying
- "Continuity in government" scheme

the contras and drugs coming north to the United States. The CIA during this period was supporting Panamanian president and drug lord Manuel Noriega. Meanwhile, the FBI was spying on over 130 progressive groups opposed to the Central American war, and there were at least eighty-five unexplained and uninvestigated break-ins. The Reagan administration began a war on drugs with disastrous results, including the corruption of police and government officials. There was also a bizarre scheme for "continuity in government" that proposed the unconstitutional takeover of government in time of crisis.

George Bush
- Iran-contra cover-up
- BCCI cover-up
- S&L cover-up

George Bush, the first ex-CIA operative and director to be elected president, presided during an extensive cover-up of the Iran-contra affair. Also under Bush, the lid was kept on the more embarrassing aspects of the BCCI scandal. Most of those involved in the S&L scandals went unpunished as well. Other individuals and corporations picked up distressed property at fire sale prices while the taxpayers footed the bill.

Bill Clinton
- Whitewater

Administration officials, the Clintons, and their friends were involved in complex and sprawling scandals growing out of Arkansas mob politics. Involved were financial misdeeds, drug running, abuse of FBI files, illegal campaign contributions, and obstruction of justice.

The problem is far from being just one of Washington's. As our lives become more regulated, we increasingly rely upon professionals to keep ourselves out of trouble. As we do so, we start to lose the sense of self-capacity essential to a vibrant citizenry.

We end up dealing not only with professionals but with layers of professionals—the doctor who sends us to the specialist, who must then have treatment approved by the insurance corporation.

In this maze we begin to lose confidence, and we stop noticing obvious things. For example, medical researchers often give one group of patients a placebo and compare the results with those receiving a test drug. As it turns out, sometimes some of those given the placebo get better. The medical industry calls this the placebo effect. And what exactly is the placebo effect? Simply improved health that occurs through some mechanism not yet discovered and

> If economists could manage to get themselves thought of as humble, competent people, on a level with dentists, that would be splendid.
>
> —Lord Keynes

approved by the medical industry. It is, in other words, an *unprofessional* cure.

Another sign of professional autocracy can be seen in state and local governments' introducing or tightening professional licensing requirements at the behest of trade associations. For example, when in recent years more and more women started to work, a number went into the home decorating business. The Washington City Council soon passed regulations for the home decorating business. And who asked it to do this? The newly launched home decorators? Defrauded consumers? Citizens endangered by hazardous mauve accents? No, it was the preexisting decorating industry, which saw the neophytes as a threat.

HOW BEAU BECAME AN EXPERT . . .

Beau Ball was an intern from Duke University who came to work one summer when I was editing an alternative newspaper. I told him, "All I want you to do is to find out everything you can about the Board of Zoning Adjustment. I guarantee you that by the time you go back to college you'll know more about the BZA than all but a handful of people in town." Not too many weeks later Beau wrote an article on what he had found. Within a couple of months two members of the BZA resigned. Beau, it turned out, had learned a lot.

There is an even more important reason not to prostrate oneself before the god of professionalism, and that is that professionals are often wrong. Every great political disaster from Vietnam to the S&L crisis to Bill Clinton's health care program had its roots in the thinking and planning of some country's most highly touted experts and professionals.*

Harvard, considered the intellectual Valhalla of America by some, has

---

Professionalism these days often seems more a cultural description than an indicator of proficiency, especially when those talking about it are speaking of themselves. It suggests a manner of packaging—rather than doing—work, one that is expensive, impersonal, and aloof but not necessarily competent.

scored something of a hat trick in this regard. Its liberal arts faculty was deeply involved in the planning and execution of the Vietnam War; its business school helped promulgate the values associated with the worst 1980s business practices (and the current economic dysfunction of America), and its Kennedy school of government has been a major source of postmodern political managers of the sort responsible for many of the problems described in this book.

This is not to say that experts are not useful. As Emerson noted, a shoemaker is good at what he does because he does nothing else. The same may be said of a lawyer or an economist. This knowledge can be of immense use. Nor is it to say that facts, experience, and understanding do not matter. Far from it. Rather it is to argue, firstly, that if you use experts, you want to be sure that they are on your side. All expertise is filtered through the prejudices, beliefs, culture, and presumptions of those who possess it. For example, one reason it is so difficult to get economic policies that benefit ordinary people is that ordinary people can't afford to hire economists. Corporations and governments can.

Some things to do

1. Fix your country or your community, not the "system."
2. Don't say you can't beat city hall until you've tried. And then tried again, using a new idea.
3. Think of new solutions, not new rules.
4. Don't make it uncomfortable for others to offer new ideas.
5. Don't worry about political labels. Be ahead rather than left or right.
6. Don't blame the weak for trouble caused by the strong.
7. Don't do the same thing over and over again and expect anything different to happen.
8. Think laterally. Imagine the solution you want, and then figure out how to get there. Experiment.
9. Don't be afraid of making mistakes along the way.
10. Use your experts, not theirs. If you can't find an expert, become one yourself.

The second point is that over and over again, intelligent and thoughtful citizens have caused social and political change by seeking out their own facts and developing their own solutions. Even when a renegade economist or a community-oriented architect or a passionate scientist has been of assistance—and one often has been—the effort has typically also depended upon people whose basic skill has been that of well-informed, deeply committed community members who knew how to educate themselves.

Finally, keep in mind that after all the facts are in, democracy still requires the blending of the self-interest of its citizens in a constructive and harmonious fashion and that you are the world's greatest living expert on your own self-interest.

An American Parts List

33 million pounds of snack food for Super Bowl Sunday

7,142 journalists accredited to the Senate and House press galleries (13 for each member of Congress)

96,000 hospice volunteers

11,500 radio stations

33,000 school jazz bands

200 government workers to accompany Vice President Gore on a trip to Russia

4. How to stay free

Hanging on to democracy in good times and bad

About the most important job of a democracy—next to serving its people—is to make sure it stays a democracy.

This is a lot harder than many people think. Forms of government don't have tenure, and governments that rely on the consent of the governed—rather than, say, on tanks and prisons—particularly require constant tending.

Unfortunately many Americans either don't understand or have come to ignore this basic principle. As things now stand, we could easily become the first people in history to lose democracy and its constitutional freedoms simply because we have forgotten what they are about.

They also thought they were free

How could it happen? Here's how a college professor, in another country and in another time, described it:

> What happened was the gradual habituation of the people, little by little, to be governed by surprise, to receiving decisions deliberated in secret; to believing that the situation was so complicated that the government had to act on information which the people could not understand, or so dangerous that, even if people could understand it, it could not be released be-

cause of national security. . . . The crises and reforms (real reforms too) so occupied the people that they did not see the slow motion underneath, of the whole process of government growing remoter and remoter.

. . . To live in the process is absolutely not to notice it—please try to believe me—unless one has a much greater degree of political awareness, acuity, than most of us ever had occasion to develop. Each step was so small, so inconsequential, so well explained or, on occasion, "regretted."

. . . Believe me this is true. Each act, each occasion is worse than the last, but only a little worse. You wait for the next and the next. You wait for one shocking occasion, thinking that others, when such a shock comes, will join you in resisting somehow.

. . . Suddenly it all comes down, all at once. You see what you are, what you have done, or, more accurately, what you haven't done (for that was all that was required of most of us: that we did nothing). You remember those early meetings of your department in the university when, if one had stood, others would have stood, perhaps, but no one stood. A small matter, a matter of hiring this man or that, and you hired this one rather than that. You remember everything now, and your heart breaks. Too late. You are compromised beyond repair.

This quote is from a remarkable book about Nazi Germany written by Milton Mayer in the 1950s. *They Thought They Were Free* (University of Chicago Press) examined not the horrific perversions but the horrible normalcies of the times. Mayer summed up his own experience this way:

Now I see a little better how Nazism overcame Germany. . . . It was what most Germans wanted—or, under pressure of combined reality and illusion, came to want. They wanted it; they got it; and they liked it. I came back home a little afraid for my country, afraid of what it might want, and get, and like, under pressure of combined reality and illusions. I felt—and feel—that it was not German Man that I had met, but Man. He happened to be in Germany under certain conditions. He might be here, under certain conditions. He might, under certain conditions, be I.

We too think we are free. But let's review the bidding. Here are some restrictions on American freedoms that are less than a generation old, each instituted, we were told, to protect us from a danger, a crisis, or a threat to national security:

> Black schoolchildren in Prince Georges County, Maryland, are being taught by the police how to behave when stopped or arrested. It is assumed by both school officials and the cops that it will happen.

❏ Roadblocks as part of random searches for drivers who have been drinking or using drugs
❏ The extensive use of the military in civilian law enforcement, particularly in the war on drugs
❏ The use of handcuffs on persons accused of minor offenses and moving violations
❏ Jump-out squads that leap from police vehicles and search nearby citizens
❏ Much greater use of wiretaps and other forms of electronic surveillance
❏ Punishment before trial such as pretrial detention and civil forfeiture of property
❏ Punishment of those not directly involved in offenses, such as parents being held responsible for the actions of their children, employers being required to enforce immigration laws, and bartenders being made to enforce drinking laws
❏ Warrantless searches of persons and property before entering buildings, boarding planes, or using various public facilities
❏ Closing of public buildings or parts of buildings to the public on security grounds
❏ Increased restrictions on student speech, behavior, and clothing
❏ Increased mandatory use of IDs
❏ Increasing restrictions on attorney-client privacy
❏ Greatly increased government access to personal financial records
❏ Loss of a once widely presumed guarantee of confidentiality in dealings with businesses, doctors, accountants, and banks
❏ The greatest incarceration rate of any industrialized country in the world
❏ Mandatory sentencing for minor offenses, particularly marijuana possession

> Random traffic stops of blacks are so frequent that the drivers are sometimes said to have been stopped for DWB—driving while black.

❏ Increased surveillance of employees in the workplace
❏ Laws in eleven states that make it a crime to suggest that a particular food is unsafe without a "sound scientific basis" for the claim

- ❏ Increased use of charges involving offenses allegedly committed *after* a person has been halted by a police officer, such as failure to obey a lawful order
- ❏ Widespread youth curfews
- ❏ Expanded definition of pornography and laws against it
- ❏ Greatly increased use of private police forces by corporations
- ❏ Persons being forced to take part in lineups because of some similarity to actual suspects
- ❏ Loss of control over how personal information is used by business companies
- ❏ Eviction of tenants from homes where police believe drugs are being sold
- ❏ Public housing projects' being sealed to conduct home-to-home searches
- ❏ Use of stereotypical profiles (including racial characteristics) to justify police searches
- ❏ Seizure of lawyers' fees in drug cases
- ❏ Warrantless searches and questioning of bus, train, and airline passengers
- ❏ Random searches of school lockers
- ❏ Random searches of cars in school parking lots
- ❏ Increased number of activities requiring extensive personal investigation and disclosure
- ❏ Lack of privacy in transactions such as video rentals or computer use
- ❏ Video surveillance of sidewalks, parks, and other public spaces
- ❏ Involuntary drug testing increasingly used as a prerequisite for routine activities, such as earning a livelihood and playing on a sports team
- ❏ Steady erosion by the courts of protection against search and seizure

Drawing the line

Over just a few decades the practices listed above have become part of "the slow motion underneath" America—little changes each "worse than the last, but only a little worse."

Is the analogy unfair? Are the procedures described above merely the necessary results of a complex, modern society? The inevitable result of a war on drugs?

To find out where you would draw the line, go back over the list of items above and ask yourself of each: Was this step necessary? Wise? Democratic?

Now here are some further measures that have been proposed, or are incremental extensions of existing restrictions, or may come about thanks to advancing technology. Which ones do you feel cross the line? At what point would you take a public stand on any of these?

- ❏ Video surveillance of public bathrooms
- ❏ Strip searches of persons matching terrorist or drug courier profiles at airports and bus and train stations
- ❏ A national ID card encoded with any or all of the following: medical information, credit history, employment record, arrest and driving record
- ❏ Checkpoints at the edges of selected neighborhoods
- ❏ Random identification checks of pedestrians by police officers
- ❏ Curfews for adults in high crime areas
- ❏ A computer data search before you would be permitted to board a plane
- ❏ Daytime curfews for youths
- ❏ Random street frisks for weapons
- ❏ Mail covers: recording by the Postal Service of suspicious names and addresses on envelopes
- ❏ Mail surveillance: opening of suspicious mail by the Postal Service
- ❏ National database assembling medical, credit, criminal, and other records in easily accessible format
- ❏ Mandatory fingerprinting or ID chip implantation for purposes of positive identification
- ❏ Incarceration in "public health centers" for those who fail mandatory drug tests required for drivers' licenses or school attendance

The right to be wrong

The major bulwark of freedom in our country is the Constitution. Many of the liberties we still enjoy did not, however, spring unchallenged from the womb of that document. Rather they were the product of protests, education, and litigation, often over long periods of time.

After being won, such freedoms tend to be taken for granted. People lose the memory of why a battle was fought and how hard it was to win. Daniel Webster warned in 1837 that the danger to the country was not from a foreign foe but from the "inattention of the people to the concerns of their government, from their carelessness and negligence." Thomas Jefferson put it even more bluntly during the Revolution: "From the conclusion of this war we shall be going downhill. It will not be necessary to resort every moment to the people for support. They will be forgotten, therefore, and their rights disregarded. They will forget themselves save in the sole faculty of making money, and will never think of uniting to effect a due respect for their rights. The shackles, therefore . . . will be made heavier and heavier, till our rights shall revive or expire in a convulsion."

Sometimes people believe in civil liberties, but mostly for themselves. Some feminists have attacked the 1st Amendment for permitting pornography, forgetting that the modern women's movement was built in part on the success of the 1960s free speech movement. Some blacks have attacked the protection of hate speech, even though such a protection works for both Louis Farrakhan and David Duke. And it has become fashionable for some academics to ridicule the Constitution as the work of dead white guys interested only in protecting property, although most of these academics have never been beat upside the head by a cop.

Because people of differing views often lose interest in liberties when they don't work to their own advantage, groups like the American Civil Liberties Union are frequently criticized for defending what Walt Kelly once described as the basic American right of people to make damn fools of themselves. The list following shows some of the freedoms that have been constitutionally established by the Supreme Court just in the past few decades thanks to the ACLU and others. It's a good reminder that while you were doing your thing, someone has been looking after you.

> Two hundred and twenty years after the signing of the Declaration of Independence, the *New York Daily News* asked 40 people on the street what happened on July 4, 1776. Only 9 got it right; almost all of them were either schoolchildren or foreigners.

A FEW RIGHTS A FEW PEOPLE HAVE WON FOR YOU IN THE SUPREME COURT

1932: The right to be protected by the Constitution even in state and local courts

1935: The right not to have your ethnic group excluded from a jury

1937: The right not to be arrested simply for attending a meeting of a peaceful but unpopular group

1938: The right to distribute literature without a permit

1939: The right to assemble in public spaces, such as streets and parks

1940: The prohibition of racially based exclusion from party primaries

1946: The limiting of the post office's power to ban "offensive" material

1948: The outlawing of restrictive real estate covenants based on race and origin

1949: The right to give a speech that some find offensive

1952: The right to produce or view a movie that some consider sacrilegious

1954: The outlawing of segregated schools

1958: The right to travel

1962: Freedom from state-sponsored praying

1963: The right of poor people to be represented in court

1964: The right to have a lawyer after being arrested

1964: The right of the press to criticize public officials robustly without fear of libel charges

1965: The right of married people to use contraceptives

1966: The right to be informed of your rights and to remain silent following an arrest

1966: The right of elected officials to criticize U.S. foreign policy

1967: The right not to have to sign a loyalty oath in order to obtain public employment

1967: The right to be protected under the Constitution if you are a young person

1967: The right to marry someone of another race

1968: The right to teach and learn about evolution

1968: The right not to be discriminated against if you are a child born out of wedlock

1968: The right to receive welfare benefits for children living with single parents

1969: The right to speech that does not directly incite imminent lawless action

1969: The right of free speech for students

1972: The right of women to be protected under the 14th Amendment

1972: The right of unmarried people to use contraceptives

1973: The right to an abortion

1974: The right of a student to receive a notice and a hearing before disciplinary action is taken

1975: The right of mental patients not to be confined indefinitely on the basis of illness alone

1986: The right to use profanity toward a police officer in the course of an investigation

1989: The right to symbolic free speech, such as flag burning

1994: The right to post political signs in the windows of your home

1996: The right of gays to equal protection under the law

Use it or lose it

The lawyer brought a copy of a book on drug legalization to the bookstore counter.

"That looks interesting," said the clerk.

"Yeah," replied the attorney, "a lot of people think this is the right way to go."

"Makes sense."

"Would you join an organization that supported legalization?"

"Oh, no, I wouldn't want the government to get my name."

Does the government compile lists of people opposed to the drug war? We don't know, although certainly government agencies have compiled such lists in the past. But in this case it really doesn't matter. The fact that the bookstore clerk believed they might has the same effect as if it were actually the case. A sort of voluntary repression has set in; what *might be* becomes as important as what *is*.

Every time an American decides that it is too dangerous to exercise a freedom, that freedom is diminished.

Thus the first rule of staying free is to act free.

Over the years many people have forgotten this. During the 1950s some of the country's most important leaders—from President Eisenhower to the heads of universities and prominent liberals—allowed themselves to be cowed by Senator Joseph McCarthy and other anti-Communist vigilantes. In doing so, they contributed to many decent people's being badly hurt.

On the other hand, a few people stood up to McCarthy and his ilk. Among the most effective were not the longtime civil libertarians—despite their steadfast efforts—but the sort of people who might well have stayed on the sidelines, as so many do today. People fortunate enough not to have to worry about the problem personally. Yet.

These people included a highly respected broadcast journalist, Edward R. Murrow, who spoke out for decency even as the networks were blacklisting other journalists for their views. They included conservative politicians such as George Aiken and Margaret Chase Smith, whose New England sense of integrity was outraged by what was happening. They also included a bow-tied Boston establishment lawyer named Joseph Welch whom Americans watched on TV being brought to tears and disgust as Senator McCarthy made an underhanded attack on one of his young associates.

Today, as then, there is a shortage of such voices. The media in particular have become unwilling to challenge the status quo, participating instead in what Spengler called the "terrible censorship of silence."

But there are important exceptions, such as government or corporate whistleblowers. Here are people who, simply because they tell the truth about their governments or employers, have been assigned to psychiatric treatment, threatened with dismissal, had security clearances revoked, been ostracized on the job or physically endangered. Among them, Pentagon analyst Ernest Fitzgerald, who was fired for revealing major aircraft cost overruns; senior government scientist Aldric Saucier, who was dismissed after finding $3 billion in duplicative Star Wars studies; and Karen Silkwood, who may have lost her life for pointing out egregious nuclear safety hazards. Here are some of the hidden heroes and heroines of democracy. They remind us that if they can take such risks, the least the rest of us can do is to act like a free people.

Understanding your warranty

The second rule for staying free is to know your rights.

When representatives of the American people met in 1787 to form what they called "a more perfect union," they drew up a sort of warranty agreement—a contract between the people and the government they were creating. They called it the Constitution. Back then you didn't have to explain why such an agreement was important. After all, the country had just fought a war against a government that had made a lot of bad laws without asking anybody. People didn't want it to happen again.

The Constitution created a new kind of government, one that did not draw its legitimacy from force and intimidation but from the people themselves and from the places in which they lived. The powers of the federal government, as it says in the 10th Amendment, are those delegated to the United States by the Constitution. Everything else belongs to the states or to the people.

Lawyers tend to make the Constitution sound far more complicated than it is. They also fail to tell you that it is not just a legal document but a political and a moral one and that your opinion about it counts too.

Polls suggest, however, that Americans are woefully uninformed about the Constitution. According to one survey, three and a half times as many Americans can name the Three Stooges as can name three Supreme Court justices.

This is one reason why it's been so easy to chip away at the rights the Constitution contains. In fact, however, the important aspects of the Constitution are easier to understand than, say, the rules for the NFL player draft or free agentry and salary caps.

The best rights you've got

Here, for example, are the most important guarantees the Constitution makes to you:

- ☑ You can say what you want.
- ☑ You can pray what you want or not at all.*

*The founders couldn't put everything in the Constitution, so they left a lot of what ifs to the courts. The courts have ruled, for example, that you can't yell, "Fire!" in a crowded theater un-

☑ You can gather peaceably with others.

☑ You can complain to the government and ask for redress of your grievances.

☑ You, your house, your papers or property may not be subject to unreasonable searches and seizures.

☑ You are entitled to equal protection under the laws of the various states.

☑ If you run afoul of the law, you are entitled to a long list of protections—just in case someone made a mistake or is trying to frame you, to wit:

1. You are subject only to warrants issued "upon probable cause, supported by Oath or affirmation, and particularly describing the place to be searched, and the persons or things to be seized."
2. You have to be informed of the crime with which you are charged.
3. You do not have to testify against yourself.
4. You can't be tried twice for the same crime.
5. You can't be tried for something that wasn't against the law at the time you did it. You are entitled to "due process of law."
6. You must have a "speedy and public" trial before an "impartial jury" if you are accused of a crime.
7. You are entitled to a court review of how and why you were imprisoned.
8. You are entitled to be confronted by the witnesses against you.
9. You can present witnesses on your own behalf.
10. You have the right to a lawyer.
11. You are to be free from excessive bail or fines as well as from cruel and unusual punishment.

Other rights that help

☞ **Freedom of the press:** There are other rights that average Americans do not usually exercise but that still benefit them. For example, freedom of the press. Freedom of the press, A. J. Liebling pointed out, really belongs to the person who owns one. Nonetheless, Thomas Jefferson thought this freedom so important he said, "Were it left for me to decide whether we should have a government without newspapers or newspapers without a government, I should not hesitate a moment to prefer the

---

less, of course, the theater is on fire. Nor can you use your freedom of speech to yell, "Fire!" to a mob that has its rifles pointed at the mayor. Similarly, your freedom of religion doesn't allow you to force others to say Hail Marys or to watch Pat Robertson on CBN with you.

latter." His views changed sharply after he became president. This is one of the reasons why a free press is important: so it will still be there after politicians have changed their minds.

☞ **Hidden rights:** Two of the most important amendments to the Constitution long attracted little attention. In the past few years that's changed. One of these is the 9th Amendment, which declares that simply listing certain rights in the Constitution does not mean that the people don't have others. In other words, not all your rights come from the Constitution. Some stem from what are sometimes called people's natural rights or from a long history of legal precedents known as common law. For example, the Constitution doesn't address privacy, but the common law does. Similarly, the right of juries to judge both the law and the facts comes from outside the Constitution—from court rulings dating far back into British history.

The other hidden right declares that any powers not delegated to the United States by the Constitution "are reserved to the states or to the people." Note that the powers of the United States are those *delegated*. This is from the 10th Amendment. When you hear the 10th Amendment being discussed, people are talking about the relative power of the federal government, the states, and the people.

> ### PREVIOUS RECALL NOTICES
>
> At the time the Constitution was adopted many Americans were denied its rights. Blacks, women, people who didn't own land, and the less educated were among those widely and long denied some or all of its protections, including the right to vote. Pre–Civil War free blacks in the nation's capital, for example, were still subject to apartheid types of codes requiring them to carry passes and to observe nightly curfews. It was not until 1920 that women were finally allowed to vote. And it was only in 1971 that those 18 to 20 years old were also enfranchised. The history of America in no small part has been the story of fighting to right such wrongs and trying to make the Constitution apply to everyone.

So who's really in charge?

You are. Even the powers of the president, Congress, and Supreme Court are there only because they have been delegated by the people and the states. Besides, once the powers are delegated, the Constitution neatly divides them up. The founders wanted to make sure none of the branches of government gained too much power over you.

The most dangerous thing any politician can say about your rights

When politicians or journalists say that a constitutional right must be *balanced* by something else, they are really talking about reducing or eliminating that right. In fact, the rights listed in the Constitution are not bargaining chips but permanent guarantees.

Lately politicians and the media have also taken to talking about "rights and responsibilities," as though free speech and free religion and not having cops raiding your house without a warrant were privileges we citizens get only when we're well behaved. Don't believe them. Your constitutional rights, to borrow a phrase from the Declaration of Independence, are "unalienable."

Of course the country will work a lot better if you vote in every election, help out in your community, and are nice to your neighbors, but these virtues aren't necessary in order for you to be protected under the Constitution. You can be a grouchy, selfish couch potato making crazy calls to talk shows and still have the same rights as the most faithful volunteer at the local church.

Selling city hall

There are ways that democracy can be lost other than through a direct assault on the Constitution. One of the most traditional methods for replacing or weakening democracy is to corrupt it.

Corruption isn't necessary illegal. If I were to make a $1,000 contribution to a political committee established to aid some member of Congress, no one would say that I had engaged in bribery. Yet in truth the only difference between a bribe of $1,000 to that congressman and a campaign contribution in the same amount is that the latter is legal.

We not only don't pay enough attention to legal corruption but tend to put far more emphasis on who is being corrupted than on who is doing the corruption.

Dead Americans	Live Politicians

I believe there are more instances of the abridgment of the freedom of the people by gradual and silent encroachments of those in power than by violent and sudden usurpations.

—James Madison

Housing Secretary Henry Cisneros, responding to criticism of plans to allow public housing searches without a warrant, said that "[b]eyond ideology, beyond partisanship, beyond fine legal distinctions," there is a demand for an end of violence.

The office of America is to liberate, to abolish kingcraft, priestcraft, caste, monopoly, to pull down the gallows, to burn up the bloody statute-book, to take in the immigrant, to open the doors of the sea and the fields of the earth.

—Ralph Waldo Emerson

Freedom is about authority. Freedom is about the willingness of every single human being to cede to lawful authority a great deal of discretion about what you do.

—NYC Mayor Rudolph Giuliani

As nightfall does not come at once, neither does oppression. . . . There is a twilight when everything remains seemingly unchanged. And it is in such a twilight that we must be most aware of change in the air—however slight—lest we become unwitting victims of the darkness.

—William O. Douglas

When we got organized as a country and we wrote a fairly radical constitution with a radical bill of rights, giving a radical amount of individual freedom to Americans, it was assumed that the Americans who had that freedom would use it responsibly. . . . What's happened in America today is too many people live in areas where there's no family structure, no community structure and no work structure. And so there's a lot of irresponsibility. And so a lot of people say there's too much personal freedom. When personal freedom's being abused, you have to move to limit it. . . .

—President Bill Clinton

While it is beyond the scope of this book (or most major religions) to end political corruption, here are a few hints on how you can keep payoffs limited to a little sex and payola and not have them destroy all our freedoms and rights.

How to keep corruption in check (& out of the Constitution)

> It's the dangest thing I ever saw. As majority leader you can't keep the money from coming in.
> —House Majority Leader Richard Armey (R-TX)

1. Hit the corrupters at least as hard as the corruptees. The real danger in corruption is what the bribe buys, not the soul of the bought politician (which probably never was in that great a shape anyway).

2. The worst corruption tends to be legal; therefore hardly anyone notices it. Remember that *corrupt* not only means "dishonest" but also means "without integrity." In most jurisdictions the latter is not a violation of the law.

3. Just because the corruption is legal doesn't mean you have to accept it. Martin Luther didn't—and so helped reform a little church-run protection racket known as indulgences.

4. Simply because corruption is bad, don't assume all reforms are good. Early-20th-century housing reformers, for example, would conduct midnight raids on tenements to expose overcrowding, and Common Cause helped give us PACs.

5. If forced to choose between minor corruption and major incompetence, take the former. It's cheaper and easier to live with.

6. Favor corruption that is well distributed—that gets down to the street—over that which only favors a few. Thus reform zoning policies before you worry about parking tickets.

Economic freedom counts too

So far we've mainly been talking about political freedom. But economic freedom is important too. The American Revolution was an economic as well as a political victory, triumphing over a system in which only the nobility and a few large merchants held economic power.

> The late Senator Paul Douglas had a good ethical rule for himself. He would accept only gifts he could eat or drink within 24 hours. Thus a pint of whiskey was okay, but a quart was too much.

The definition of economic freedom at the time was quite different from that used by today's corporate chief executive seeking yet another tax break. Early free Americans widely believed that one was entitled to the "fruits of your labor" and no more. They opposed the concentration of property because it would allow property owners to seize political power.

During the entire colonial period only about a half dozen business corporations were chartered. In the first 20 years after the Revolution only about 150 corporations were chartered. Each of these charters required that the corporation be in the public interest.

Early free Americans were not capitalists (the word hadn't even been invented). The Constitution was written for people and not for corporations. Free enterprise was not mentioned in it.

These early Americans were, however, deeply commercial. One reason for this was that commercial activity allowed them to break free of the social and economic restrictions of a British economy based on nobility and monopoly. Americans didn't want to work for such a system; they wanted to work for themselves. And they weren't concerned about competition because there wasn't much.

The rise of the modern corporation in the late 19th century represented a countercoup against these values of the American Revolution. It dramatically undermined both political and economic freedom, corrupted politicians, and ransacked national assets. It replaced the feudalism of the monarchy with the feudalism of the corporation.

Perhaps the most important event occurred 110 years after the launching of the American Revolution. In 1886 the Supreme Court ruled that a corporation was a person under the 14th Amendment and entitled to such constitutional protections as those of free speech.

With this fiction the Court helped boost the corporate takeover of America. The 14th Amendment had been clearly written to protect the rights of newly freed slaves, yet by the 1930s—fifty years later—less than one half of 1 percent of 14th Amendment cases coming before the Supreme Court involved blacks, and more than 50 percent involved corporations seeking its protection.

As persons, corporations could inject themselves fully into civic life (such as influencing campaigns and politicians) while repelling public interference in their own affairs. They could construct barriers on civil liberties grounds against efforts to control their rapaciousness and greed. Many of these rights

HOW STATES ONCE CONTROLLED CORPORATIONS

The purposes for which every such corporation shall be established shall be distinctly and definitely specified in the articles of association, and it shall not be lawful for said corporation to appropriate its funds to any other purpose.

—State of Wisconsin, 1864

The charter or acts of association of every corporation hereafter created may be amendable or repealed at the will of the general assembly.   —State of Rhode Island, 1857

[Legislators shall] alter, revoke or annul any charter of a corporation hereafter conferred . . . whenever in their opinion it may be injurious to citizens of the community.

—State of Pennsylvania, constitutional amendment, 1857

that corporations secured by law came even as blacks and women were still struggling toward full enfranchisement.

During much of the past century Americans went along with the rising power of corporations because these companies provided higher incomes and ever-increasing jobs. But about 20 years ago, these two conditions began to disappear. Part of today's political tension stems from a growing concern over the rising political power of big corporations even as their social and economic contribution to America declines.

Privatizing democracy

Another easy way to diminish democracy—one that has become immensely popular in the 1990s—is to privatize it. Of course that's not quite how it's described. Pro-ponents speak of privatizing *services* or privatizing *government,* but what they often mean is making a corporate entity out of what was formerly part of democracy.

This trend has occurred with the media hardly noticing the political erosion involved. In fact, in the lexicon of politics and press these days, the citizen has been reduced to a mere *consumer* or *taxpayer,* terms that wipe out the fundamental notion of *ownership* of government by the public. The citizen, it is now widely suggested, only pays and is served; the citizen no longer decides.

Privatization inevitably creates an additional barrier between the citizen and whatever is being done. To be sure, cities have long contracted out such services as trash pickups, and that often works pretty well, but what is now happening is not only the contracting out of services but the contracting out of democratic control. There is an immense difference between letting the Biggo Corporation collect your garbage and letting it teach your kids. When a school system contracts with a private firm to run its schools, it not only is transferring the power to teach and administer but is delegating its own power to decide democratically how these things should happen.

The media has been a major cheerleader of privatization. It, in particular, likes a new form called the business improvement district. The idea is to designate a special district, usually downtown, in which a special assess-

A REALLY SIMPLE RULE ON PRIVATIZATION

Ask the following question:
Is this something about which citizens should have a say?
If the answer is yes, don't privatize.

ment is applied to local businesses and their tenants to support such programs as new lighting, security patrols, and planting. There are now about 1,000 of these districts across the country with budgets as high as $10 million a year.

In these districts, voting on directors and their policies may be weighted on the basis of tax payments, thus favoring the largest commercial interests even though the owners may not even reside in the city involved. In many cases owners of major property not only get to decide but can pass on the fees they approve to their tenants. Residents and business tenants tend to have little or no say.

Such districts, in essence, apply the principle of corporate voting—the more money you have, the more votes you get—to public decisions. Even in the early days of the Republic—when the franchise was limited to property-owning white males—each voter still got only one ballot.

And after you've taken over downtown, where are you going now?

Just as the ads say, to Disney World.

Disney has outdone downtown business districts by purchasing a whole town. Lake Buena Vista, Florida, has only 40 citizens, some 30 million visitors, and only one major business, Disney World. By creating its own jurisdiction, Disney has revived the 19th-century notion of the company town and eliminated the need for local democracy. As Joshua Wolfe Shenk wrote in the *American Prospect,* "At stake is the control of public space. Americans may have so despaired of government that they are ready to concede authority over whole communities to private corporations. But, then, who insures democratic accountability? And where does corporate power end? ... The 'secession of the affluent,' as Robert Reich has called the growth of private communities and private governments, is an acceptable solution to our problems only if democracy is irredeemable."

Letting corporations run wild

The privatization of democracy is just part of the damage done by a post-1980 era of permissiveness toward corporations. Some of the other results:

- Declining real incomes for working Americans despite record corporate profits
- The S&L scandals
- The incorporation and industrialization of health care
- The emigration of jobs and businesses abroad
- The rise of multinationals and a decline of corporate loyalty toward the United States
- The dismantling of union agreements
- The de facto repeal of antitrust laws
- Growing assaults on environmental and health regulations
- The co-optation of the Congress, White House, and both major political parties to the service of major corporations
- Deep political corruption fueled by corporate lobbying and contributions

Why has all this happened so easily? One reason is that the politicians themselves have been privatized. If you compare what members of Congress receive in government salary with what they get from business in campaign contributions, you might easily conclude that your representative is a corporate employee. You would not be all that far off.

There is a name for what has happened. It is corporatism, a system in which the state exists primarily to advance the interests of its largest corporations, which in turn direct the economy and national priorities.

Just as communism represents an extreme form of socialism, so corporatism represents an extreme form of capitalism.

America did not invent corporatism. That honor really belongs to Mussolini's Italy. Here's how historian Adrian Lyttelton describes Mussolini's approach: "Industry was ordered to form 'a common front' in dealing with foreigners. To avoid 'ruinous competition,' and to eliminate inefficient enterprises . . . the values of competition were to be replaced by those of organization: Italian industry would be reshaped and modernized by the cartel and trust."

We had a less flattering term for what the Italians were about: fascism. Al-

Public Space	Private Space
On public property you have the right of free speech. So does a corporation.	On the corporation's property only the corporation retains the full right of free speech.
While in the town square, you are protected not only by the Constitution but by a broad range of other laws, such as those ensuring civil rights.	While you are in a shopping mall that frequently replaces the town square, your constitutional and legal rights are greatly restricted.
If you live in a town or village—a real community—you share with other voters broad powers over what happens and who carries it out.	If you live in a developer's "community," nearly all decisions will be made by the developer's company.
In a traditional downtown, decisions such as tax policy are made by the voters and the people they elect. All these persons are residents of the town.	In the new privatized business districts sprouting up around the country, decisions (including special assessments) are made by commercial taxpayers. Residents and tenants may get no vote, and the business owners need not live in the community

though we usually equate fascism with a particularly evil form of political tyranny, its roots were in an economic system. Lyttelton in fact defines fascism as "a product of the transition from the market capitalism of the independent producer to the organized capitalism of the oligopoly."

Sound familiar?

Restoring economic democracy

This use of the government of all for the enrichment and aggrandizement of few is a revolution. . . . These sovereign powers . . . have been given by you and me, all of us, to our government to be used only for the common and equal benefit. Given by all to be used by all, it is a revolution to have made them the perquisite of a few.

—Henry Demarest Lloyd,
speaking in the 1890s
to a crowd in Cook County, Illinois

In the last few years there has been growing support for a simple and direct notion: that we should correct the egregious error the Supreme Court made when it declared corporations to be persons. This could be achieved by passing a constitutional amendment inserting some words clarifying that the equal protection clause of the 14th Amendment is meant to apply only to living human beings.

In America's new economic circumstances, such a change would raise an issue that is no longer academic or quixotic. The battle over such an amendment would force Americans to educate themselves about the corporate usurpation of our rights. It would help citizens learn the huge difference between economically productive commercialism and corporate feudalism.

Some things to do to stay free

1. Act like a free American.
2. Know your rights.
3. Know where you will draw the line and take a stand.
4. You don't have to like other Americans; you do have to be decent to them.
5. Don't let anyone "balance" your rights with anything. Your rights are inalienable.
6. Don't let your politicians sell your democracy to private business.
7. Amend the Constitution to make clear that corporations are not entitled to rights designed for individual citizens.

An American Parts List

105,000 injured in-line skaters
each year

177 billion annual pieces of mail

208,000 stolen laptop computers
in 1995

$31,000 to support one American household for a year

$35,000 to get Cokie Roberts to give a speech to the
Junior League in Fort Lauderdale, Florida

20 million members of
12,400 health clubs

5. How to count the votes right

& other amazing tricks you can play on the system

How the system is rigged

1. We use a voting system called winner-take-all. The winner need only be first and not necessarily the choice of the majority of voters. In fact, we have had 17 presidential elections won by less than a

    > The two major parties spend their time trying to please every-one and end up pleasing only a few of us.

    majority—4 since 1960. In the 1992 election, for example, the only state in which any candidate won a majority was Arkansas.

2. We tend to elect legislators by single-member districts. One of the problems with this can be seen by imagining that every congressional seat in the country was won by the Blue party—but each by only one vote. Under winner-take-all, the Blues would gain all the seats in the House, and those voting for the Yellows and the Greens and the Browns would not be represented at all.

You don't even have to imagine. In 1912, with the GOP splitting its votes with the Bull Moose party, the Democrats won 12 of the 13 Indiana House seats with only 45 percent of the vote. In 1918 the Democrats again got 45 percent of the vote, but this time—against a united Republican party—they lost every seat. That's an extreme case, but it shows one of the major flaws of our system: We provide representation only to those who win.

Here are some other things wrong with our system:

- **It discriminates against minorities and minority views.** For example, if representation in Congress after the 1992 election had been proportional to the presidential vote, there would have been at least 80 Perot supporters in the House of Representatives. Our system keeps minorities out of public office—and not just ethnic minorities either. When new voting methods were introduced in southern communities as a result of voting rights lawsuits, not only blacks but Republicans started showing up on government
bodies.

- **It can also discriminate against the majority.** First-past-the-post elections with multiple candidates may not reflect the majority's will, but rather only which minority got the most votes.

- **It gives too much importance to personalities and too little to issues.** With only two parties that pretend to represent the country's entire political spectrum, it is nearly impossible for either party to propose a coherent program or even a new idea. Too many compromises have to be made. Instead of discussing substantive matters, candidates turn to negative advertising or to issues deliberately designed to polarize the citizenry. This, it turns out, is also an easy way to appeal to swing voters who don't really care for either candidate.

- **It works against peaceful change.** The genius of a well-working democracy is its ability to adapt to new social conditions and values. The tumult of democracy is a happy substitute for more violent solutions. Winner-take-all elections, however, discount deeply alienated minority voting blocs. These voters are urged to take their complaints to the voting booth, yet when they get there, they discover their votes aren't worth anything.

What to do about it

PROPORTIONAL REPRESENTATION

Fortunately there are some things we can do about it. For example, we could vote like most other democracies.

One of America's best-kept secrets is how strange our voting system really is. Only Britain, America, members of the British Commonwealth, and a few other countries rely on winner-take-all. In fact, to most of the world we vote the way the British drive—on the wrong side of the road.* Most countries with elections use some form of proportional representation, which means that seats in legislatures are divvied up in proportion to the votes received by each party. This includes not only most of the old democracies in Europe but the newly freed countries of South Africa and the former Soviet Union. Under PR, if the Late Night TV party were to win 18 percent of the vote, it would get about 18 percent of the seats. Under the present rules in America, parties that win 18 percent of the vote usually don't get any seats. Instead their members stay home, watch late-night TV, and get mad at the system.

> **WOMEN, MINORITIES, & PR**
>
> Using a form of proportional representation, Cambridge, Massachusetts, has consistently elected people of color to its legislative bodies—even though the city is only 14 percent black. In 1993 a black man was elected mayor on the first ballot (the only candidate so elected), and two black women were among the six members elected to the school committee.
>
> In 1995 women won 41 percent of the seats in the Swedish legislature after threatening to form a new party if they weren't better represented on party slates. In Germany women won 39 percent of the seats elected by PR (but only 13 percent of the district seats). Democratic newcomer South Africa had a legislature that was 24 percent female in 1995. Meanwhile, our House of Representatives had only 11 percent women, and the United States ranks 24th out of 54 Western democracies in the percentage of women in the national legislature.

Strange as proportional representation may seem, it has a history in this country going back to the Progressive Era, when nearly two dozen cities used it—including New York, Sacramento, and Cleveland. It disappeared

---

*A consistent beneficiary of winner-take-all elections was Margaret Thatcher, who conducted her whole revolution without the Conservatives ever getting more than 45 percent of the vote.

> Politics may be noisy, disorganized, and corrupt, but it starts to look better when you compare it with riots, bombings, and civil war.

not because it was ineffective but because the urban power brokers didn't like it.

In 1915, when Ashtabula, Ohio, adopted the system, the local paper enthused, "The dries and the wets are represented; the Protestants and the Catholics; the business, professionals, and laboring men; the Republicans, Democrats, and Socialists; the English, Swedes, and Italians are represented. It would be hard to select a more representative council in any other way."

One of the great advantages of proportional representation is that it is fair. In South Africa it has provided representation not only to the dominant party but to the white minority and black opposition parties. Ninety-nine percent of South African voters were able to elect someone to represent them! This is one important reason South Africa's transition from apartheid was as smooth as it was.

The Germans may even have a better idea. They didn't want to give up district elections entirely. After all, it's useful having a legislator elected to look after your community. So they came up with a very democratic solution: They mixed their systems.

> In America, says election scholar Douglas Amy, "You have the right to vote—you just don't have the right to be represented."

In Germany half the legislature is elected by district, just like here in the United States. The other half is elected by PR nationwide. The PR winners are selected in such a way that the whole parliament is proportional to the national vote.

Here's how it works: Let's say that the Blue party wins 20 percent of the district seats, but 35 percent of the national vote. After the district winners have been selected, the rest of the seats are filled in such a way that the Blues have 35 percent of the entire parliament.

Opponents of PR make a number of arguments against it. For example:

- **It is too complicated.** But are Americans dumber than Germans? How come South Africans, including the illiterate, were able to understand it so easily in what was for many their first election ever?
- **Having a lot of parties leads to political instability.** Heard of any coups or political crises in Germany or Sweden lately? In fact, in a recent

Swedish election, 86 percent of the voters turned out. Besides, most countries use some sort of minimum threshold (such as 5 percent) before a party is entitled to any seats.

☞ **Well, look at the Italians.** The Italians have had a lot of governments since World War II, and proportional representation sometimes gets the blame. To the extent that PR caused instability it was largely because the Italians adopted an unusually low threshold for winning seats. Any party getting just 1 percent of the vote could be seated. But there was less instability than it appeared. For example, during 51 successive governments, there were only 13 prime ministers, with the Christian Democratic party a key member of each coalition government. Gianfranco Pasquino, political science professor at the Università degli Studidi, Bologna, has even argued that given the consistent influence of the Christian Democrats, the stability of personnel, and the continuity of policies, the frequent turnover represents "a sort of safety value for a political system without alternation."*

PREFERENCE VOTING

What about elections for single posts like mayor or governor? Clearly proportional representation doesn't work here.

There is, however, a system that does, and it is in use in places such as Ireland and Cambridge, Massachusetts. It's called preference voting.

In the United States we typically elect winners for single positions using a system called first-past-the-post. Whoever gets the most votes wins.

For example, if there were four candidates in a race for mayor, the winner could theoretically be elected with 25 percent of the vote plus a few ballots. Three quarters of the city's voters might detest the winner, but it wouldn't matter.

Preference voting is one of the best ways to create a better consensus. In some states runoff elections are used, but the results in these are

> Under our system if you lose, you lose big. Our system creates a lot of unhappy losers.

---

*In 1993 Italy—in the midst of massive corruption scandals, the collapse of the Christian Democrats, and hoping to end party factionalism—moved to a system in which 75 percent of the seats are elected by district. The results so far have included a shift from party to regional factionalism, the silencing of opposition parties in some regions, and fewer women being elected for the district seats. In the 1996 elections Italy had the lowest turnout since World War II.

typically distorted by the far lower turnout in the second round of voting.

Under preference voting, you get to rank your choices. Then, if no one gets a majority, the candidate with the lowest number of votes has his or her ballots redistributed according to supporters' second choices. If no one still has a majority, another redistribution occurs with the ballots of the next lowest-ranked candidate and so forth. One way this system protects minorities (either cultural or political) is by encouraging voters to select their favorite candidates without reference to the chance of winning. Let's say that you are vehemently opposed to the construction of a new bridge. Only one candidate shares your view, and she stands little chance of winning. You can rank this candidate first and then be more pragmatic about your second choice. Since major candidates know this is happening, they go after second-place as well as first-place votes instead of writing off minority views, as often happens in winner-take-all. They may even modify their position on the bridge in order to get second-place votes.

The system can also be used—as it is in Cambridge—for multiseat elections, in which case it becomes a form of proportional representation. The rules are more complicated, but they work and are specifically designed to ensure that varied interests are proportionately represented in legislative bodies.

There are still other variations, such as a system known as approval voting, in which you don't rank your choices but just vote for as many candidates as meet your approval. Others prefer cumulative voting in multiseat contests, a system in which citizens can concentrate all their ballots on one candidate or spread them around as they wish. Each system has its advocates—often argumentative ones—but each scheme represents a major improvement on the current system. As the *Los Angeles Times* put it, "Mathematicians do not agree on the best system, but they have no problem pointing their fingers at the worst—the plurality system used in most U.S. elections."

> [Legislatures] should be an exact portrait, in miniature, of the people at large.
>
> —John Adams

LARGER LEGISLATURES

You're probably already thinking, Oh no, not more politicians. At other times, however, you've probably also said that politicians have lost touch with the people. So consider this:

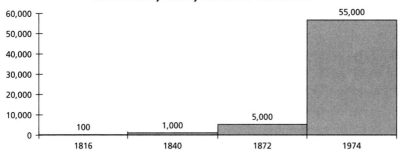

Number of voters for each Columbus, Ohio, council member

Year	Number of voters
1816	100
1840	1,000
1872	5,000
1974	55,000

- The United States hasn't increased the size of the House of Representatives since 1910. Meanwhile, the population of the country has almost tripled.
- We have one of the smallest national legislatures per capita among the world's democracies.
- A member of the House represents 15 times as many people as did members of the first Congress. Many large city legislators today represent more people then did the first members of the House. A state senator in California represents more people than does a member of the U.S. House of Representatives.
- In the 1880 Garfield presidential election, when politicians were far more accessible, about one in five northern voters took an active part in a campaign organization, and 83 percent voted!

Could it be that one big problem with our politics is that we have too few, rather than too many, politicians? Most of us are glad—for all our complaining—to have elected politicians do our work for us. At the same time we want them to be far more responsive. One good way to have this happen is to bring them closer to us by electing more of them.

UNRIGGING THE SENATE

The Constitution requires two senators per state—no matter how large or small. As a result the 21 smallest states have 42 votes in the Senate even though when combined, they don't match the population of California with its two votes. The Senate so poorly reflects the country's ethnic character that if it were a private club, you'd want to resign from it before running for office. If it were a school system, it would be under court-ordered busing. Here are some ways to change this undemocratic situation:

- ✏ **Increase the number of states.** Making new states out of current metropolitan areas, for example, would help end the antiurban, antiminority bias in the Senate. Whenever anyone suggests turning California into two or three states or making the District of Columbia a state, many laugh at the idea. Yet statehood has happened 37 times since the original 13 colonies joined together. What's more, the founders made it easy. Giving blacks and women the vote or approving an income tax required constitutional amendments. But a new state can be created just by majority vote of Congress and the president's signature. A new state can be created out of an existing one if the state legislature also approves. This is why Maine is no longer part of Massachusetts and why there is a West Virginia as well as a Virginia.

> We tend to take the vote for granted. New democracies don't. When Eritrea had its first referendum (on succession from Ethiopia), 99.8 percent of the voters cast ballots. One of them, reported Tim Wise of Grassroots International, was a 60-year-old man who walked all night from his village and then waited 10 hours in the desert sun for his turn. Another was a woman who delivered her newborn outside the voting station.

- ✏ **Change how the Senate is elected.** *New Yorker* editor Hendrik Hertzberg has proposed a constitutional amendment to give each state one senator and have the other half of the Senate elected nationally by PR in staggered terms. This would make the Senate elections similar to the German mixed system.
- ✏ **Use preference voting.** Even with no new states and no constitutional amendment, preference voting could be introduced in Senate races to make sure the results more fairly reflect a state's consensus.

ENDING THE BIGGEST BALLOT FRAUD

The biggest ballot fraud in America takes place long before election day. It consists of the rules that determine who gets on the ballot in the first place and how many signatures you need to join them. These rules are controlled

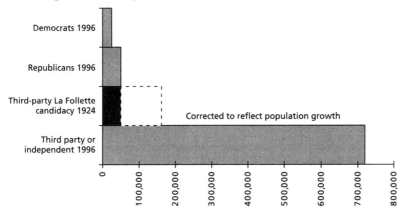

Signatures required to run someone for president

by federal, state, and local bodies run by appointees of the two major parties and are consistently and specifically designed to protect these parties' duopoly.

The fraud continues during the campaign itself, when candidate "debates" arbitrarily exclude third-party candidates from the discussion.

OTHER WAYS TO MAKE THINGS FAIRER

☑ **U.S. House:** Only a congressional law—nothing in the Constitution—says that House members have to be elected by district. If the size of the House were increased by 50 percent, many states could convert easily to a PR system. Right now a mid-size state like North Carolina could take an incremental approach and adopt preference voting in four three-member districts or could go to a

DIRECT DEMOCRACY

Will Rogers said once that "anything important is never left to the vote of the people. We only get to vote on some man; we never get to vote on what he is to do." Initiative and referendum laws help correct this problem. While initiatives and referenda sometimes reflect voter cruelty and shortsightedness, this is no more true than in the case of representative government. These measures tend to cut both ways and have been used against gays in Colorado and to fight timber clear-cutting in Maine. Such laws may not improve the quality of voters, but they do empower them.

statewide PR system for its 12 House members. Big states like California would be perfect candidates for the German-style mixed system. The beauty of using PR in the House is that it would offer a way out of the dilemma created when the Supreme Court voided districts drawn in weird ways in order to guarantee minority representation. For example, in the case of North Carolina, whose bizarre district lines were rejected by the Court, PR advocates have come up with a proposal that, on the basis of typical voting patterns, would be likely to produce at least three black representatives *without* gerrymandering.

☑ **State legislatures:** Some states could adopt PR systems for their legislatures with a simple statute change; others would require state constitutional amendments.

Illinois, in fact, used cumulative voting, a semi-PR system, from 1870 to 1980, and as recently as 30 years ago a majority of state legislators were elected from multimember districts.

Washington and New Jersey now have two-member districts and could implement mixed-member PR without redrawing current districts. Maryland, New Hampshire, and other states with multimember districts could use preference voting to elect legislators within current district boundaries.

☑ **Cities and counties:** Preference voting could be easily instituted for mayoral elections. The use of traditional PR is somewhat limited because it depends on party slates and many city elections are nonpartisan. Multiseat preference voting for councils is complicated by safeguards to ensure broad representation, but computers have made vote counting a cinch.

☑ **Organizations:** Preference voting is an ideal system to elect the leadership of organizations from a local PTA to national religious denominations. Hundreds of universities, trade unions, and nonprofit organizations use preference voting in Britain, as do a growing number in the United States.

☑ **U.S. president:** As in all single-winner contests, a president cannot be directly elected by PR. But preference voting would work well for such races. And even without a constitutional amendment abolishing the electoral college, reforms can be made in the way it functions. For example, the electoral votes of states could be allocated by proportional representation, an idea that was supported by both Franklin Roosevelt and Richard Nixon.

THINKING SMALL

Liberals are afraid to criticize big government because they think it makes them sound like Republicans. In fact, the idea of *devolution*—having government carried out at the lowest practical level—dates back at least to that good Democrat Thomas Jefferson. Even FDR managed to fight the Depression with a staff smaller than Hillary Clinton's and World War II with one smaller than Al Gore's. And conservative columnist William Safire admits that "in a general sense, *devolution* is a synonym for 'power sharing,' a movement that grew popular in the sixties and seventies as charges of 'bureaucracy' were often leveled at centralized authority."

The modern liberals' embrace of centralized authority makes them vulnerable to the charge that their politics is one of intentions rather than results—symbolized by huge agencies, like the Department of Housing and Urban Development, that fail miserably to produce policies worthy of their names.

Conservatives, on the other hand, often confuse the devolution of government with its destruction. Thus, while the liberals are underachieving, the conservatives are undermining.

In fact, a sensible and democratic devolution of power should be high on the American repair list. The question must be repeatedly asked of new and present policies: How can these programs be brought close to the supposed beneficiaries, the citizens? And how can government money go where it's supposed to go?

Because such questions are not asked often enough, we find huge disparities in the effectiveness of federal programs. For example, both Social Security and the earned income tax credit function well with little overhead. In such programs the government serves primarily as a redistribution center for tax revenues.

On the other hand, an environmentalist who ran a weatherization program told me that she figured it cost $30,000 in federal and local overhead for each $1,600 in weatherproofing provided to a low income home.

Similarly, a study of Milwaukee County in 1988 found government agencies spending more than $1 billion annually on fighting poverty. If this money had been given in cash to the poor, it would have meant more than $33,000 for each low-income family, well above the poverty level.

Even when you don't want to devolve power out of the federal government—and in many cases you don't—the programs themselves can be brought closer to people. Some agencies already are quite decentralized, including U.S. attorney offices, the Coast Guard, the National Park Service, and the delivery of mail. In such cases the federal government is represented by a small unit (or even an individual, such as your postal carrier) with considerable autonomy within a defined turf.

The principle could be applied to other agencies. Why not, for example, have 50 state directors for the Department of Housing and Urban Development, each (as with U.S. attorneys) approved by the state's senators and each given a budget, a menu of programs, and considerable autonomy in how to handle them? I would wager that there would be at least two results: (1) Citizens would have a better idea of what was going on in federal housing programs, and (2) the programs would get better.

MAKING DEMOCRACY AN AMATEUR SPORT

The single most frustrating problem facing those who wish to make elections fairer is how to control the money spent on them.

A few politicians do manage to beat the campaign money system. Representative Andrew Jacobs, in 14 successful runs for the House, spent less money than many of his colleagues blew in a single campaign. He won one race with $8,250 and in another urged supporters not to send him contributions—he had some left over from the last time. Jacobs would tell his In-

---

INSTRUCTING YOUR POLITICIANS

When U.S. senators were selected by state legislatures, some of these bodies would send mandatory voting instructions to their representatives in Washington. In such cases senators might speak out against a bill and then have to vote for it. In 1913 the Constitution was amended to provide for the popular election of U.S. senators, but the right of instruction remains in the constitutions of 16 states. In Massachusetts, for example, instructions to state legislators can be put on the ballot.

The idea of instruction was backed by James Monroe, Patrick Henry, Henry Clay, and Abraham Lincoln. And John Adams promised, "The right of the people to instruct their representatives is very dear to them, and will never be denied by me."

---

diana voters, "You get a big spender in the campaign, you get a big spender in Congress. It's habit-forming, spending other people's money."

But Jacobs was virtually one of a kind. And so we have attempted a variety of campaign finance reforms. The problem with these is that they often fail to achieve their goals. For example, political action committees and the Federal Elections Commission were meant to clean up politics; they clearly haven't. Many reformers favor limited public financing, yet we already have some public financing of presidential elections, and private money continues to play an enormous role.

The Center for Responsive Politics points out that presidential candidates raise most of their money very early. In four elections since 1980, for example, the candidate who raised the most money by January 1 of election year became the party's nominee. Then there is the soft money given to political parties which is supposed to be used for general party purposes but in fact becomes part of the candidates' piggy banks. In 1992 both major parties raised significantly more in soft money than their presidential candidates did in federally regulated contributions.

> There are only two things that are important in politics. The first is money and I can't remember what the second one is.
> —Ohio political boss and U.S. Senator Mark Hanna, 1895

Some argue vehemently that any limits on campaign spending are a violation of the First Amendment. They say money makes political free speech possible and note that Eugene McCarthy's 1968 effort—which led to LBJ's not running for reelection—could not have happened without the support of big individual contributors. Further, they point out that challengers generally need more money than incumbents do.

> Girlie, do you have any idea of what you're getting into?
> —A senior House colleague to first-term Representative Linda Smith, who was proposing campaign finance reforms

On the other hand, it makes little sense to say that a poll tax is an unfair levy on the exercise of democracy and still effectively charge a half million dollars to win a seat in Congress. (A close race costs $677,000, but you can lose for just $238,000.) Besides, as American University Law School Dean Jamin Raskin has pointed out, we don't think of a john's giving money to a prostitute or a politician's being bribed as an expression of free speech.

Some say the answer is to ban, or not accept, PAC money. But the bulk of

At the other end of democracy from the traditional town meeting is the still-experimental notion of blending technology and political deliberation. Teledemocracy, as it's called, includes voting by phone, mail, or computer as well as holding electronic town meetings.

For example, in 1992 the Liberal party of Nova Scotia elected its party leader by phone tally—with nearly half of all party members participating. Several other regional parties in Canada have since followed suit.

As with any new technology, there is a wealth of uncertainties, philosophical issues, and problems. Nonetheless, with these experiments the potential of cyberdemocracy is becoming increasingly clear.

money going to winning congressional candidates comes from individuals. In presidential races the effect of PACs is even less. In the 1992 election PACs accounted for only 1 percent of total funding.

There are other problems. Not only is political office in this country bought, but it is paid for by an extremely few people. The residents of New York City's Upper East Side contributed more to congressional campaigns around the country in 1994 than all the residents of 21 states. In 1990 one tenth of 1 percent of the voting-age population accounted for 46 percent of all the money raised by congressional candidates. And campaign limits often don't help because they make politics more attractive to the rich, who, thanks to the 1st Amendment, can use their own funds in campaigns without limitation. The irony is that in protecting the 1st Amendment, such rules ignore the 14th, which provides for equal protection under the law.

In the end the most sensible goal would be to have public financing and free television time so plentiful that they would heavily discount the effects of private money. This can be done for surprisingly little. Consider, for example, what our current system of private campaign financing really costs citizens in *public* dollars. The table below shows what just six industries gave to congressional candidates and in soft party money in the 1992 campaign and what they got back (with our tax dollars) in subsidies and tax breaks. Spending just $10 in public funds for each voter—probably enough to fund all local, state, and federal contests—would cost a minuscule fraction of what politicians now spend in our tax dollars to pay back their big contributors in just six industries.

Talk about getting a bang for your buck

	Political Contributions*	Subsidies & Tax Breaks*
Waste management	$3	$300
Mining	$1	$2,000
Natural gas	$3	$4,300
Coal	$1	$8,000
Oil	$23	$8,800
Nuclear energy	$0.1	$11,000

*In millions. I would like to have displayed all this using a graph, but the difference between what the industries gave and what they got was so great that the contributions wouldn't have shown up without a magnifying glass.

MEANWHILE, HOWEVER . . .

Since public financing may not be in place in time for the next presidential election, here are a few other things we can do in the meanwhile:

- We can change political culture as well as laws. Politicians would like us to talk about family values. Let's talk about their values instead. We can vote against candidates who are on the dole. We can write letters to the editor and call talk shows. Local, state, and national citizen groups can come together and establish codes of conduct for candidates and officeholders.
- We can support legislative efforts that are steps toward full public financing.
- We can work to reform state and local elections. One of the ways change happens is for a few states or localities to lead the way. Why not yours?
- We can pressure parties to reform finance rules for their own primaries, which they can do without any new legislation.

THE ULTIMATE REVENGE

Another good way to buck the system is to run for office yourself. If the office is low enough down the political food chain, money won't even matter as much. For example, a well-regarded small-town council member ran for the state legislature. She was trounced by a 24-year-old neophyte. His secret: He personally visited every Democrat in town.

One of the easiest ways to get into politics is to run for something nobody else wants. The posts are there. For example, in 1995 no one filed to run for the office of mayor in 131 Iowa towns or for 81 of the state's city council seats.

You can learn a lot even by losing, and if you run a good campaign, voters can learn from you. A Green, Tian Harter, ran for the Sacramento City Council. He got only 22 percent against a popular incumbent. Afterward Harter did his own election analysis and found some interesting things:

> [Politics] is a series of unsentimental transactions between those who need votes and those who have money.
>
> —Arkansas chicken king Don Tyson

- In precincts where people knew about his previous campaign, where he had been endorsed by local leaders, or where the incumbent had offended these leaders, his total went up to about 35 percent.
- He got an additional 8 to 15 percent of the vote in areas where his main issue, bus service, was important to the voters.
- He got an extra 8 percent just by walking the precinct once early in the race. In places where he campaigned late he did even better. The best results were in precincts he walked within one to three weeks of the election.
- Where he did nothing, his total went down to 10 to 12 percent.
- In one precinct he got 45 percent. He doesn't know why.

Harter concluded, "I know that [the voters] are doing the best they can with the information they have. No one gives away their vote. People just make what appears to be the best choice with the information they have when they go into the voting booth. I wouldn't have understood that without campaigning."

BUILDING LITTLE
DEMOCRACIES AROUND US

One of the best ways to revive democracy in our country is to make sure that every organization, church, school, and club meeting is run according to its principles.

> The town meeting: the strongest of all citadels of civil liberty, the purest of all democracies.
> —From the official seal of Danvers, Massachusetts

A great model for such gatherings is the New England town meeting. This is a far cry from the undemocratic political talk fests pioneered by Jimmy Carter and pursued since by every cynical politician and every public affairs TV producer desperate for a program idea.

Ken Bresler, who has written a primer on Massachusetts town meetings, notes that "one reason that Massachusetts colonists revolted against Great Britain was the British attempt to ban most town meetings except by permission. In 1774, British soldiers tried to stop a Salem town meeting in progress, but the citizens barred the door of their town house and continued to meet." And on April 19, 1775, the Lexington militia held an impromptu town meeting to "consult what might be done," as the local minister put it, about the advancing British.

New England town meetings were—and are—serious democratic business. Says John Gould in his book *Town Meeting:* "Absolute independence characterizes town meeting. No one tells a Yankee how to vote, no one dictates, and only another Yankee can persuade."

In Massachusetts, towns of fewer than 6,000 people must have open town meetings; larger communities can elect representatives to do their work for them. Both are chaired by moderators—a nicely descriptive title far less pedantic than chairperson or facilitator. All the town's registered voters can speak at either meeting. In an open town meeting they also vote. In a representative town meeting they vote for officers and meeting members, who in turn carry on the business of the town.

James Weaver, a political science professor at Marymount College, studied the town meeting of Friendship, Maine. According to the *Maine Times,* he concluded that "all things considered, it appears democracy is alive and well in Friendship, due largely to faith in the town meeting as the citizen's legislature. Those who attend a town meeting may debate and vote on the important items, and may even choose to postpone decisions indefinitely, which, in the opinion of one prominent fisherman, is a 'useful way to keep the people in charge.' "

Another early American model for reaching democratic decisions comes from the Society of Friends. The Quakers have always conducted their business on the basis of consensus. While the concept seems risky and time-consuming to those who have not observed or participated in it, people all over the country are adapting consensus as they come to realize that majority voting is often insufficient—or even alienating—in our increasingly diverse communities. The beauty of consensus is that people feel better after reaching it, for in its wake is clear evidence that one has done the best possible under the circumstances.

Instead of a vote, there typically comes a call for consensus expressed by a question such as "Are there any concerns remaining?" If there are concerns, the group attempts to work them out or amend the proposal under consideration. If there are still problems, some members of the group may agree to "stand aside" on the issue—in other words, to retain their concerns but not block the decision.

Non-Quaker groups often modify the approach, using something less than full consensus. Or they may attempt consensus and, if it bogs down hopelessly, turn to conventional voting. Seeking supermajorities (such as requiring approval by two thirds of the body) is another way to force the majority to deal with minority concerns.

At the very least, attempting to reach consensus on issues, and using voting only as a last resort, are great ways to create decisions without creating losers.

Lani Guinier tells a story that illustrates well the danger of traditional winner-take-all voting even in seemingly nonessential situations. A high school class used majority voting to choose music for the prom. Since the class was heavily white, the only songs chosen were those the white students liked. The black students ended up boycotting the prom. An alternative system— such as consensus or preferential voting—would have led to a happier outcome.

To make meetings democratic, decent, yet still productive, you can also:

- Stress common ground. Get people looking for things they can agree on rather than fight about.
- Hide your copy of *Robert's Rules of Order*. At least try simple fairness and civility before building parliamentary mazes.
- If an issue starts to bog down a meeting, have each side select a representative, have the representatives choose a mediator, and ask all three to leave and try to reach a consensus.
- Use preference voting for the selection of officers and boards.
- If you are trying to draft a program or policy, break up into small groups dealing with specific aspects of the matter. List every idea on newsprint. Then give the participants three or four small colored stickers with their initials on them. Let them place these stickers on the ideas they most favor. Then, as in preference voting, drop those ideas with only one sticker, and let those who supported them move their stickers elsewhere. Continue until consensus is reached. The physical activity alone helps ease some of the tension that can develop on such occasions.
- Use fishbowl negotiations. Have each small group select a representative. Have the representatives gather in a circle with their group members behind them. While only the representatives are allowed to negotiate the final decisions, their group members can stop them at any time for a caucus. Everything is done in front of everyone else; that's how it gets its name.
- Meetings can turn otherwise decent people into demons, the succinct into the pedantic, and the normally direct into the convoluted. A moderator or chair with a sense of humor and fairness can prevent a lot of misery. Everyone else can help by acting like real people. Representative Sonny Bono, frustrated by a 12-hour House committee meeting that was going nowhere, told his staff to buy 15 pizzas and bring them to the back of the room. As the aroma drifted toward the dais, the committee quickly ended its unproductive proceedings and adjourned for midnight pizza.

An American Parts List

23,000 new car dealers, 1,000 of whom won't haggle over price

2,833 new school dropouts each day

1,579 hours a year of TV watching for each American

33 million trees for sale at Christmastime

26 gallons of coffee annually for each American

6,670 barbecue restaurants

6. How to count the money right
A totally unauthorized guide to the economy

A few things they don't tell you

THE NATIONAL DEBT IS REALLY NOT THE SAME AS YOURS.

While there are similarities, the parallel between personal and public finances is often misleading. For example, when you borrow money from the bank, you owe it to someone else, and you know there will be trouble if you don't pay it back. But when America borrows money, it borrows mostly from itself. America is not about to foreclose on America. Besides, everyone who owns a savings bond, has money in treasury bills or holds publicly invested CDs is a creditor of the United States as well as a debtor. Most pension plans get some very secure income thanks to the federal government's owing them money. This makes government debt very different from yours. Abraham Lincoln thought it so clear that he overoptimistically concluded that citizens "can readily perceive that they cannot be much oppressed by a debt which they owe themselves."

ALL DEBT IS NOT THE SAME.

When we talk about the national debt, we tend to make no distinction between types of national debt. There is an immense difference between going into debt for capital investments like schools and bridges and going into debt

THE MAKING OF A MIDDLE CLASS

The [1940s] wartime economy allowed millions of Americans who had been on relief to get back on their feet. . . . The society of a few haves and a multitude of have-nots had been transformed. Because of the greatest—indeed, the only—redistribution of income downward in the nation's history, a middle class country had emerged.

—Doris Kearns Goodwin in *No Ordinary Time*

THE UNMAKING OF A MIDDLE CLASS

A recent study of fourteen industrialized countries found that America had the smallest middle class relative to the whole population. The biggest middle class was found in that den of socialist iniquity, Sweden. On the other hand, the United States had the second-largest upper class relative to total population (next to Ireland) and the largest low- and modest-income class. Says economist Lester Thurow: "Probably no country has ever had as large a shift in the distribution of earnings without having gone through a revolution or losing a major war."

to pay current operating costs. That's why a bank will lend you money to buy a house but not for dinner and a movie. Our national budget makes no distinction between buying schools and buying doughnuts. It should.

CUTTING GOVERNMENT SPENDING TAKES MONEY *OUT* OF THE ECONOMY.

There are plenty of good reasons to be frugal with public funds, but "putting money back into the economy"—a popular political cliché—isn't one of them. This is because like it or not, government spending is part of the economy. A dollar doesn't really know whether it's being spent publicly or privately. Or whether it last came out of profits or taxes.

In some cases, in fact, a public dollar can do much more good for the economy than a private one. For example, government is generally required to buy domestic products and hire domestic workers, while private corporations are under no such restrictions. Even more dramatically, a billion or two spent on public works is far better for the economy than using the money to allow one baby boomer to buy another's corporation. On the other hand, purchasing a tank that just sits on a military base doesn't have anywhere near the same spin-off economic effects as spending the same amount of money on pizzas to go.

REVENUES ARE PART OF BUDGETS TOO.

Lost in the great balanced budget mania of the 1990s was a fact obvious to anyone in business: A really good way to improve your books is to increase your revenues. For government, this simple notion has gone out of style. The assumption has become that the only way to reduce the deficit is to cut expenses. But just as a business needs customers, our country needs thriving citizens and companies to keep it going.

CUTTING THE BUDGET DEFICIT DOES NOT REDUCE THE NATIONAL DEBT AT ALL.

The government's deficit represents the federal budget shortfall in a particular year; the national debt is the sum of all these deficits—less any money that has been repaid. Therefore cutting the deficit only slows the growth of the national debt; it does not reduce it. To cut the debt, the government would have to create a surplus and apply it to the national debt. At that point politicians and citizens would start hollering for a tax cut, and everyone would probably forget about the national debt.

CUTTING THE BUDGET MAY NOT EVEN CUT WASTE.

Few of us like to see the government waste money. Yet while Americans have been sold on the notion that cutting the deficit will cut waste, it seldom does.

A FEW THINGS THAT HAPPENED WHILE POLITICIANS WERE BUSY CUTTING THE DEFICIT

- The Clinton administration paid $12,280 for a spare C-17 cargo jet door hook that originally cost $389. A two-by-four-inch aluminum hinge for a door to the plane's air-conditioning system leaped from $30.60 in 1992 to $2,187 just a few years later.
- The Pentagon-subsidized Shades of Green Resort, a 20-acre hotel complex at Disney World used for morale purposes, was costing us $27 million annually.
- The cost *overrun* on Boston's new highway tunnel—funded 85 to 90 percent with federal money—rose to $8 billion.
- It was learned that the Bureau of Indian Affairs couldn't account for $2.4 billion it spent between 1973 and 1992, or $1 out of every $7 flowing through tribal trust funds during this period.

In part this is because the same politicians who claim to be budget slashers also have a bunch of pet projects they want funded. Multiply that instinct by the number of congressional members and you've got 535 big problems.

Further, a lot of waste is so well concealed that it takes a Government Accounting Office investigation or a public interest group to uncover it. Unfortunately such stories typically make one day's news and then are forgotten.

There is also waste that is so well hidden that no one even knows how it happened. At the Pentagon, when the military knows money has been spent but doesn't know on what or who authorized it, it is called a problem disbursement. By the mid-nineties there were tens of billions of dollars worth of problem disbursements on the military's books.

Finally, journalist Kevin Phillips has pointed out, the politicians who talk the loudest about balancing the budget often are really far more interested in other things, such as reducing taxes, or helping Wall Street, or slashing programs they don't like for political reasons. A balanced budget becomes just an excuse to get these other things done.

CUTTING BUDGET DEFICITS CAN BE HAZARDOUS.

Cutting deficits can easily have unfortunate side effects. Investment manager Warren Mosler has closely studied the relationship between the economy and deficits. He finds that with remarkable consistency, reducing the deficit as a percentage of the

TALE OF TWO ERAS

In the 15 years prior to the Reagan era, family income rose 16 percent for the poorest fifth of the nation and 23 percent for the richest fifth, so everyone came out ahead. In the 15 years after Reagan's inauguration, the poorest fifth saw its family income decline 13 percent while the income of the richest went up 17 percent.

gross domestic product leads shortly to a slowdown in economic growth or even to a recession. Further, he could find no cases where cutting the deficit has increased the rate of economic growth. As Mosler explains it: "The noble attempt by Congress to balance the budget will result in a weaker economy. . . . Every time the budget deficit, as a percent of GDP, drops the growth rate drops a few quarters later. It is only after the deficit begins to expand again the economy recovers. The historical correlation is 100%."

Ironically, something similar frequently happens to corporate profits as the relative role of the deficit declines, suggesting that the budget cutters on Wall Street may be not only wrong but masochistic as well. So how do you know when your deficits are too high? Economist Robert Kuttner thinks it's when the debt grows much faster than the economy. That happened during the Carter years. But, says Kuttner, you can deal with this "without a forced march to absolute balance." A business spurt or a reduction in interest rates, for example, can mean more tax revenues without cutting the budget at all.

CUTTING THE NATIONAL DEBT CAN BE DISASTROUS.

History suggests that cutting the national *debt* can be even worse than slashing the deficit. Mosler notes that we have only had six periods of sustained debt reduction. These sustained reductions, over 5 to 14 years, ranged from 27 percent to 100 percent of the national debt. For example, the national debt was reduced by a third in the 1920s. Andrew Jackson even managed to produce a surplus of $440,000. Each time the national debt has been significantly reduced, a major depression has followed. There are no contrary cases.

Still more things they don't tell you about the economy

THE GROSS DOMESTIC PRODUCT IS PRETTY GROSS.

The gross domestic product is a measure of the amount of money changing hands in the United States. When you hear or read about "economic growth," people are talking abut GDP.

It's important—and misleading. For example, the gross domestic product doesn't give a damn about what happens to the money that changes hands. For all the GDP cares, it can be used to build a church or for a Klan rally. As long as money's moving, it's considered good for the country. I know that's

weird, but that's the way economists think.

In an article for the *Atlantic Monthly*, reformers working on an alternative measure, the genuine progress indicator, wrote:

By the curious standard of the GDP, the nation's economic hero is a terminal cancer patient who is going through a costly divorce. The happiest event is an earthquake or a hurricane. The most desirable habitat is a multi-billion-dollar Superfund site. All these add to the GDP, because they cause money to change hands. It is as if a business kept a balance sheet by merely adding up all "transactions," without distinguishing between income and expenses, or between assets and liabilities.

In the same spirit, the *Wall Street Journal* figured that the O. J. Simpson trial added about $200 million to the economy or more than the annual GDP of Grenada. Prozac adds another $1.2 billion.

The GDP also doesn't take into account the massive amount of productivity that isn't paid for at all: the voluntary economy. Just as lawyers try to get us to view the world through adversarial lenses, so economists encourage us to view the world as a place in which the only activities that matter are those that are reimbursed. It is a world without cooperation, altruism, or even barter. It is a world without parents, friends, or neighbors doing things for one another. It denigrates the bulk of human activity—especially that of women, who have traditionally functioned outside the formal economy and do about half of the world's real work without getting paid for it.

The genuine progress indicator (GPI) adds things up differently:

- Household work is valued at what it would cost if you had to hire someone to do it.
- The money people spend to deter and punish crime is assumed to be a cost to society rather than an asset.

- Also listed as costs are auto accidents, water filters, and other environmental protection devices.
- The depletion of natural resources is assumed by the GPI to be a liability, whereas it is currently treated as a gain.
- Overwork—working two jobs or longer hours—is considered a cost to society.

More than 400 economists from across the spectrum have endorsed the idea of new economic indicators. It's still being worked on, but maybe soon you'll be getting quarterly updates on the GPI. Meanwhile, even those of us who don't like the GDP continue to use it while trying to remind people that it's only about spending money and not about whether the money's doing anyone any good.

THEY'RE NAIRU MOMS, NOT WELFARE MOTHERS.

NAIRU stands for the "nonaccelerating inflation rate of unemployment." This is the rate of unemployment many economists say is required to keep us away from inflation. Our government agrees with them.

This emphasis on inflation may be explained by something the economist John Kenneth Galbraith has pointed out: The wealthy are hurt more by inflation, and the poor are hurt more by unemployment. In any case, if as a matter of national policy an unemployment rate of 5 to 6 percent is a good thing, we then need to find more than 5 million loyal people who will support this policy by remaining unemployed or underemployed. Of course, since we can't really admit that we're doing this, we end up pushing expensive and ineffective training (for jobs that corporations would like to get rid of) and workfare programs (which economists hope won't work too well), and spend a lot of time berating poor women. One letter writer to the *Washington Post* suggested that instead they deserve a postage stamp and a national holiday.

THE WORD FROM HEADQUARTERS

As employee layoffs mushroomed in the mid-nineties, a survey of 35 large corporations found that average compensation for their CEOs had risen 23 percent in 1995 to $4.4 million.

IF YOU THINK THE SOCIAL WELFARE STATE
IS BAD, CONSIDER WHAT LIFE WAS LIKE BEFORE IT.

If you reached adulthood sometime in the last 20 years or so, chances are you haven't heard much good about the social welfare state. In truth, however, public welfare and health programs, which began in the last century and accelerated in the early part of this one, brought some of the greatest economic and social advances of human history, many of which you and I enjoy and take for granted today.

Life before these programs wasn't all that pleasant. There was no Social Security, unemployment compensation, minimum wage, or meaningful occupational safety rules. It was a time of uninspected meat and milk, of unregulated medicinal drugs, of firetraps and unseaworthy vessels, and of much shorter life expectancy.

Furthermore, before public health and sanitation programs there was a tendency for city streets to be strewn with manure, garbage, rooting pigs, and an occasional dead horse.

As for those who weren't wealthy, a typical view during the Victorian era was expressed by a popular motivational speaker in some 5,000 lectures: "To sympathize with a man whom God has punished for his sins . . . is to do wrong. . . . Let us remember that there is not a poor person in the United States who was not made poor by his own shortcomings."

Even the socialists of the day didn't think that highly of the poor. Fabian Beatrice Webb in England suggested that the poor be divided into the deserving and the not deserving and that the idle loafers be subjected to "compulsory training, or military or other training . . . absorbing the whole time of the man from 6 A.M. to 10 P.M."

But when it came time to fight the Boer War, the British found that 40 percent of its recruits were unfit. The British government responded by appointing a Committee on Physical Deterioration that recommended not only free school lunches but compulsory free medical examinations. The American

> Deficit spending is legitimate when it is used to protect the future well-being of the nation. . . . [The national debt provides the only place where] households, insurance companies, banks and, not least, pension funds, including Social Security, can invest whatever assets need to be placed in the least risky of all financial instruments.
> —Economist Robert Heilbroner in the *New York Times*

Army had similar problems getting ready for World War II. In both countries school lunch programs and health care were advanced not as an act of knee-jerk liberalism but to make sure there were enough healthy men for the military.

SOCIAL SECURITY MAY NOT BE GOING BANKRUPT AFTER ALL.

Everyone's heard that the Social Security trust fund is going to go bust sometime in the next century. But only a few people have actually looked at the assumptions justifying this prediction. Doug Henwood of the *Left Business Observer* did and found that the figures assumed economic growth barely above that of the Depression years of the 1930s, half the rate of the past 75 years.

People who complain about the welfare state remind me of the man from Virginia who went to college on the GI Bill and bought his first house with a VA loan. When a hurricane struck, he got federal disaster aid. When he got sick, he was treated at a veterans' hospital. When he was laid off, he received unemployment insurance and then got a SBA loan to start his own business. His bank funds were protected under federal deposit insurance laws. Now he's retired and on Social Security and Medicare. The other day he got into his car, drove the federal interstate to the railroad station, took Amtrak to Washington, and went to Capitol Hill to ask his representative to get the government off his back.

Says Henwood: "Either the trustees are deliberately projecting slow growth to feed the pension-cutting mania, or they're expressing a deep pessimism about the U.S. economy's future. Big news, whichever it is." If the trustees' growth projections are accurate, we have a lot more than Social Security to worry about.

The Social Security and Medicare scare that has been directed at younger Americans obscures a number of other important points:

- People are going to become older and ill whether or not we make decent provisions for them. The choice for younger Americans is not whether they have to pay for the future but whether they'll pay through a planned government program or on an ad hoc and unpredictable basis— for example, having to support ill parents out of their own salaries and savings at a time not of their choosing. Further, it is probable that those now in their twenties may someday grow old and ill themselves.
- While there is great hue and cry over the possible fate of Social Security, the same Cassandras show little interest in the fact that we have only

> Number of persons in a 1996 poll who said they or someone close to them had been affected by layoffs: 72 percent.

some 40 years of proved oil reserves left. If a trust fund runs out, spending from other sources can take its place. If the wells run dry, however, you can't print more oil.

☞ University of Pittsburgh Professor Emeritus Frederick Thayer has asked why it is that we worry about the effect of the "crushing debt" on our children and grandchildren in peacetime, but not during wars, when we run up enormous deficits? Obviously, he notes, a " 'crushing burden' could have been avoided by not responding to the attack on Pearl Harbor." Instead, thanks to World War II, our economy boomed.

☞ While the demographic bulge caused by baby boomers will eventually create a much larger senior population, the figure that really matters is the total dependent population, including children. Twentieth Century Fund President Richard C. Leone has pointed out that there was once a boomer bulge among the dependent young and somehow Americans coped with that. He notes that in 1964 there were 96 young and old dependents for every hundred wage earners, but in the dreaded future of 2030, there will be only 83 per 100 (as opposed to 70 per 100 in the early nineties).

☞ Finally, one way to cover deficiencies in the Social Security trust fund is to raise the upper limit of income—currently $62,700—subject to Social Security withholding. Or tax unearned income, such as interest and dividends. Not surprisingly, the Social Security goblins never suggest that they themselves might pay Social Security taxes on the second $62,700 they earn—or even the third and fourth if need be.

YOU DON'T HAVE TO BE GLOBALLY COMPETITIVE IF YOU DON'T WANT TO BE.

Contrary to what you have heard from politicians, economists, and journalists, you do not have to become globally competitive in the first half of the 21st century if you don't want to. Here's why: Most of the economy then, as now, will be domestic. Only about 25 percent of the economy currently involves imports and exports.

One reason there's so much talk about global trade is that big corporations would like you to stop pushing so hard for things like higher wages, workplace safety, and a healthier environment. They want you to lower your sights and become more like a worker in the nonindustrialized countries. The more they succeed at this, the more globally competitive they become. You, unfortunately, just become poorer, less healthy, and not even domestically competitive.

ON WALL STREET THERE ARE PLENTY OF FREE LUNCHES BUT NO FREE MARKETS.

The carefully concealed truth is that Wall Street and corporate America hate free markets. That's why these welfare fathers keep tens of thousands of lobbyists in Washington: to protect them from the random effects of the competition they so frequently extol. That's why they invented welfare programs for multinationals such as GATT and NAFTA. That's why they have their own branch of government—the Federal Reserve—to keep the economy working the way they want it, and that's why the federal tax code is so complicated—glutted with special breaks and subsidies for "free" marketeers.

The least free of all markets is to be found at the Pentagon, where defense contractors have become so dependent on their single customer, the military, that more than a few simply wouldn't know how to survive in normal business competition.

Generally, the smaller the business, the more it resembles the great myths of capitalism. If you want to find out what free enterprise is really about, talk to a street vendor and not to a Fortune 500 executive.

And now a few true facts about money

MONEY IS INFORMATION.

While everyone talks about the economy—what we do with our money—little attention is given to the real nature of money. Money isn't only a way of storing wealth; it is also information. Money is how we measure the value of something, just as an inch is a way we measure length. David Burman explained it nicely in Canada's *Peace Magazine*:

> Imagine that you are going to have a house built. You have assembled all the materials, you have the necessary permits, have acquired the land, and

have engaged experienced and skilled workers to do the job. But when you come on the scene to see how things are going, you find that nothing has happened. The foreman responds to your look of annoyance, "Uh, sorry, we can't start."

"Why not?" you ask incredulously.

"Well, we're all out of inches. Used 'em all up on the last house down the road. Have to wait until we can get some more, maybe next week."

Absurd as this story may seem, we treat money information just this way. Despite having resources and labor available, despite will and skill, we repeatedly say that something can't be done because we don't have enough money. In fact, over the past few years it's been one of the favorite things for politicians to say. As we'll see a little later, there are much better ways to use the information that money provides us.

MOST MONEY DOESN'T EXIST.

The total federal, state, local, and private debt in this country in 1996 was around $14 trillion. The actual money supply was just under $6 trillion. So what happened to the rest of the money? Most of it doesn't exist and never did. We call this imaginary money debt. This debt is money that we (as individuals, companies, and governments) have borrowed, primarily from private sources. As Bob Blain, a professor at Southern Illinois University, puts it: "Most debt is not the result of people borrowing money; it is the result of people not being able to repay what they owed [to banks or individuals] at some earlier time. Instead of declaring them bankrupt, creditors just add more to their debt."

This new debt is called interest. Many people think the idea of the government's printing money is shameful, yet our laws permit private financial institutions to create money all the time. Every time you fail to pay off your credit card, you're letting a banker print some more money.

You're not the first, of course. For example, when the Congress met in February 1790 to figure out how to pay off the Revolutionary War debt of $75 million, Alexander Hamilton strongly advocated issuing interest-bearing debt certificates and using them as money. Congressman James Jackson of Georgia warned that this would "settle upon our posterity a burden which [citizens] can neither bear nor relieve themselves from. . . . Though our present debt be but a few millions, in the course of a single century it may be multiplied to an extent we dare not think of."

IT'S REALLY OKAY FOR THE GOVERNMENT TO PRINT MONEY.

An alternative to Congress's borrowing money to pay off the debt would have been to have created the $75 million, using its constitutional power to "coin money and regulate the value thereof." Instead Congress began a long tradition of borrowing money that—$5 trillion of debt later—many believe we can neither bear nor relieve ourselves from.

In the early 19th century the little British Channel island of Guernsey faced a smaller but similar problem. Its seawalls were crumbling. Its roads were too narrow, and it was already heavily in debt. There was little employment, and people were leaving for elsewhere.

Instead of going still further into debt, the island government simply issued 4,000 pounds in state notes to start repairs on the seawalls as well as for other needed public works. More issues followed, and 20 years later the island had printed nearly 50,000 pounds. Guernsey had more than doubled its money supply without inflation.

A report of the island's States Office in June 1946 notes that island leaders frequently commented that these public works could not have been carried out without the issues, that they had been accomplished without interest costs, and that as a result "the influx of visitors was increased, commerce

> The privilege of creating and issuing money is not only the supreme prerogative of government, but is the government's greatest creative opportunity. By the adoption of these principles, the taxpayers will be saved immense sums of interest.
>
> —Abraham Lincoln

was stimulated, and the prosperity of the Island vastly improved." By 1943 nearly a half million pounds' worth of notes belonged to the public and was so valued that much of it was being hoarded in people's homes, awaiting the island's liberation from the Germans.*

About the same time that Guernsey started to fix its seawalls the city of Glasgow, Scotland, borrowed 60,000 pounds to build a fruit market. The Guernsey seawalls were repaid in 10 years; the fruit market loan took 139. In the first part of the the 20th century Glasgow paid over a quarter million pounds in interest alone on this ancient project.

How did Guernsey avoid the fiscal disaster that conventional economics prescribed for it? First and foremost by understanding that when you build roads or seawalls or colleges or houses, you are not reducing your society's wealth. In fact, if you do it right, you are creating something that will add to its wealth. The money that was created was simply backed by public works rather than gold or "full faith and credit." It was, in fact, based on something more solid than the dollar bills in our wallets today.

---

*The cagey burghers of the Channel Islands are no longer interested in this form of financing. The islands have instead become offshore havens for major banks and for the megarich.

A 12-step program for recovery from corporatism

> Gross National Happiness is more important than Gross National Product.
> —King Jigme Sungye Wangchuk of the kingdom of Bhutan

1. **Create a local currency.** It's legal to print your own money, provided that it can't be mistaken for the government kind; the Secret Service frowns on that. In fact, says Barbara Brandt in *Whole Life Economics,* in the 1860s there were more than 10,000 different kinds of locally issued bank notes, including those issued by state banks, in use in the United States simultaneously.

After the creation of federal banking during the Civil War and the Federal Reserve System in the early 1900s, the variety of money in this country contracted. Then, in the 1930s, when communities found themselves with products, needs, skills, and labor but little money, local currencies made a comeback. Writes Brandt:

> In numerous communities, local governments, business associations, or charitable groups began to create their own money systems for local use. Local depression money came in many variations: vouchers that could only be traded in specific stores, or for specific items, and printed currencies (often called "scrip") on paper, cardboard, or even wood, which had to be spent within the community a certain number of times or before a certain date. . . . By 1933, the *New York Times* reported that one million Americans in three hundred communities were using barter or scrip systems to keep their economies going.

THE PENTAGON JOB BUST

Part of the argument for keeping a big military is the jobs it creates. But the Center for Defense Information points out that between 1987 and 1995 defense-related jobs declined by two million while employment not related to the military increased by almost 15 million.

Further, says the CDI, $1 billion in military spending creates about 25,000 jobs. The same money spent on housing would create 36,000 jobs or, in health care, 47,000 jobs.

Today there is a revival of community money—or green dollars, as it is sometimes called. In 1983 Michael Linton developed a local exchange trad-

If you want a simplified tax system, go for a thin tax rather than a flat tax. The system's complexity has virtually nothing to do with the number of tax rates—a point conservative flat tax supporters have nicely obscured. A thin tax—i.e., no longer than a page or two—could be easily achieved while still maintaining progressive taxation.

Here are two ways to improve the property tax:

1. Lower home property tax rates by broadening the property tax base. A $100,000 house is typically taxed as property, but not $100,000 in stocks or antiques. A surtax on interest income and on the insured value of non–real estate valuables would make the property tax fairer. An even simpler approach would be to lower the federal capital gains tax on real estate by the sum of all property taxes paid on it.

2. Tax empty land suitable for development at a higher rate than improvements on developed land. A number of communities have done this with good results. It discourages vacant lots and buildings and encourages more compact development. Of course ecologically important land needs to be exempted.

ing system (LETS) on Vancouver Island that created $350,000 worth of trading in its first four years. David Burman puts it this way: "LETS is as close to a biological organism as an economic system can be. . . . Low administration fees pay for daily operations entirely in green dollars. Federal dollar expenses like telephone and postage come from nominal annual fees. . . ."

In Ithaca, New York, some half million dollars' worth of local trade has been added to the economy through Ithaca Hour notes. An Ithaca Hour is based on the average local wage, about $10 an hour. Ithaca Hours have been used to buy plumbing, child care, car repair, and eyeglasses. They are accepted at restaurants, movie theaters, bowling alleys, and health clubs. As Paul Glover explains in *In Context*, "We printed our own money because we watched federal dollars come to town, shake a few hands, then leave to buy rain forest lumber and to fight wars. The local money, on the other hand, stays in our region to help us hire each other."

The Ithaca money was inspired by the success of a similar program in western Massachusetts, where in 1989 a local restaurateur, Frank Tortoriello, raised a badly needed $5,000 in 30 days by issuing scrip. His Deli Dollars drifted into the local economy and even began showing up in church collection plates.

Edgar Cahn has come up with some imaginative ways to rebuild a nonmonetized economy without even using scrip. He calls his system time dollars. For example, in one Washington, D.C., community, volunteers accumulate credit hours for a local organization through baby-sitting, cleaning alleys, and so forth. These hours are then traded for the professional legal help the organization needs. Although the participating law firm already was doing a lot of pro bono work, time dollars changed the relationship between lawyers and the community. The latter now earns assistance through its own efforts, and the firm treats the lawyers' time as billable hours.

2. **Print money for capital projects.** As the island of Guernsey found out, printing money is a sound way to fund capital projects. In the United States, the Sovereignty movement claims the support of over 3,000 city, town, and county governments and school boards, as well as five state governments, for its plan to allow states and localities to borrow money interest-free from the federal government for capital projects or to pay off existing debt. The money would be created by Congress, as authorized by the Constitution. When the money is repaid, it either could be retired from the monetary system or used to reduce the national debt.

3. **Consider high unemployment a problem.** It is not just a hedge against inflation, especially when you consider that the real unemployment rate—including those who have given up looking for work and others not counted—is double that of the published rate.

4. **Value the unmeasurable.** Economics argues that if you can't measure it, it's not important. In modern economics, altruism and cooperation are given no value; neither are do-it-yourself projects or the bulk of unpaid work done by women around the globe. Economists not only have trouble with theory but can't even add right.

5. **Create cooperatives.** Capitalism and socialism are not the only economic alternatives available to us. There is, for example, the cooperative, essentially a company in which all shareholders have an equal voice. Because cooperatives must please all shareholders and not just the big ones, and since shareholders are typically also employees, customers, and members of the community, cooperatives tend to be much more

socially responsible than the average corporation. The cooperative has had a long history in the United States, especially in rural communities, where the co-op was often the major store. According to Renate Hanauer in the journal *Deep Democracy,* 30 percent of American farmers' products are still marketed through co-ops.

Co-ops can be huge businesses. In Japan, cooperative societies have some 18 million members and 2,300 stores. Co-op Atlantic is a cooperative that is the fourth-largest regional business in the Atlantic provinces of Canada, enjoying 20 percent of the retail consumer goods market in the region. Co-op Atlantic was started 70 years ago by fishing and farming clubs. According to Jane Livingston in *Green Horizon,* "they organized study clubs to become economically literate and organized co-ops to eliminate exploitive middlemen." Since cooperative values stress equality, equity, and mutual self-help, the training to be a Co-op Atlantic manager includes learning both traditional management and the skills of cooperation. Co-op Atlantic now has more than a half million members.

6. **Encourage civic enterprise.** Civic enterprise is an alternative to corporate enterprise and to privatization. It is perhaps the oldest form of joint economic activity outside the family. Like cooperatives, it is business with a soul. It is the community coming together to do business together: to build housing, to provide electricity, even to own its own sports team. It is the opposite of what Madison, Wisconsin, Mayor Paul Soglin once called "lemon socialism"—that system favored by large corporations in which local and state governments are only allowed to get into activities that aren't profitable.

Civic enterprise can mean local public ownership, or it can mean community ownership with special rules. It can mean borrowing from local residents for local projects instead of relying on the New York bond market. Civic enterprise is why you won't see the Green Bay Packers moving out of town soon. They're owned by 2,000 mostly local residents who can't sell their shares for profit, an approach so threatening to other team owners that it has been banned elsewhere by the NFL. And there's nothing wrong with a city or a state's owning its own public utility, downtown land, or even, as in North Dakota, a bank.

An increasingly popular form of civic enterprise is the community development corporation. These institutions, primed with public and private money, are beginning to make a noticeable difference in center city communities. In one neighborhood of Washington, D.C., a CDC started with a supermarket, profits from which now help to run a nearby drug clinic. There is also the Development Corporation of Columbia Heights, which helped local resident Richard Ferguson get his ice-cream truck after a bank had turned him down, as well as assisted him to buy a three-story building and become licensed to sell ice cream at the 1996 Olympics. As Courtland Milloy wrote in the *Washington Post*: "In an area that had been one of the District's most notorious open-air drug markets, there are now new homes and a mini-mall. The mall includes the Big Wash Laundromat. It is owned by 20 working-class neighbors. . . . They formed an investment group, saved $30,000 and decided to provide their community with a badly needed facility for washing clothes." Says Development Corporation chief Robert Moore: "We have calculated that $400 million is generated in our community each year but only one percent of that money stays here. We must find more ways to make our money work for us."

7. **Revive usury laws.** Among the silent victims of the 1980s were usury laws and those who benefited from their protections. Lobbyists for lenders quietly got Congress and states to ease up on caps on mortgage interest and other loans. The results were predictable. As the *Washington Post* belatedly reported more than a decade later, "lifting caps resulted in new abuses, including 'reverse redlining'—lenders targeting borrowers in low income neighborhoods, forcing them into foreclosure with high interest rates and reselling their property."

   Banks have even come up with some novel forms of usury, such as effectively charging depositors interest on their own money if they fail to keep a certain minimum on account or bilking them at usurious rates at ATM machines, both in the guise of service charges. Banks are now engaging in practices that once only your master sergeant or neighborhood loan shark would have attempted.

8. **Create more credit unions, community banks, and lending circles.** A credit union is the financial sibling of a cooperative. Although credit unions have existed for a long time, their boom in the 1960s and 1970s unfortunately failed to survive the hostility of Reagan-era regulators. Credit unions are now often shoestring operations, limited in the types of loans they can make—mostly to small depositors. Yet they still have 63 million members and assets of over $100 billion.

   A variation called community development credit unions—while still not as free to make business loans as a regular bank—have sometimes done extremely well. In six years, for example, the Central Brooklyn Credit Union grew to $3.7 million in assets and 3,200 members.

The Central Brooklyn Credit Union also created lending circles, small groups of individuals who pool their resources and make loans to fledgling businesses. Writes David Spero: "Normally, low-income start-ups would have small chance of success, but the lending circles function as support groups and coaches, making sure the fledgling entrepreneur succeeds and repays her loan."

Where credit unions are too small or too restricted, community development banks have begun to appear. These banks are like a regular bank—only with a conscience. Does this make them risky ventures? Not necessarily. The South Shore Bank in Chicago had a loan loss rate of less than one percent on the first half billion it put out on the streets.

9. **End the corporate riot.** Runaway corporatism hurts democracy, and it doesn't make economic sense either. Job growth in America is mainly dependent upon small business—especially micro firms with fewer than 20 workers. Yet our economic planning is dedicated to the interests of huge corporations whose priorities include seeing how many more people they can lay off and how much of their business they can move overseas.

Two important leaders of the corporate reform movement are Richard Grossman and Ward Morehouse. Here are a few things they think we can do to recapture the ground lost in the corporate counterrevolution of the past century:

- Dismantle especially harmful corporations, using provisions such as the one in New York law that calls for dissolution when a corporation acts "contrary to the public policy of the state."
- Recharter corporations for limited times, subject to precise restrictions.
- Reduce the size of corporations.
- Establish worker and community control over corporate units.
- Ban specific toxic chemicals and toxic wastes.
- Cap management salaries.
- Ban the hiring of replacement workers during strikes.
- End corporate extortion and subsidy abuse.
- Ban corporate contributions to political campaigns.

How radical is all this? Not very, if you check American history. Jonathan Rowe, writing in the *Washington Monthly,* reported that before

1842 the state of Maryland chose one third of the directors of the B&O Railroad. A bank charter in New Jersey required assistance to local fisheries. In fact, until 1837, says Rowe, "every state required that corporations be chartered only for a particular type of business" and many charters automatically expired after 20 to 50 years.

10. **Encourage employee ownership.** An employee takeover at United Airlines, reported the *New York Times,* produced these results: "Sick time is down 20 percent. Grievances filed by the pilots are down 75 percent. So are worker's compensation claims. . . . When the airline wanted to renegotiate with the pilots to allow round-the-clock world service, the talks took just two days. Another telling statistic is that the list of pilots seeking jobs at United has swelled to more than 10,000 even though the airline pays less than some of its biggest rivals."

Of course nothing insulates United's 83,000 employee-owners from the vagaries of the economy or the marketplace, and some worker-owner experiments have haven't worked out at all. On the other hand, employee ownership helps dismantle unproductive corporate hierarchies, builds worker security, and deepens company loyalty.

What is believed to be the first employee stock ownership plan was created in 1937 by the publisher of the *Milwaukee Journal.* He wanted to keep the paper locally owned and independent. In an age of manic media mergers it still is. About 90 percent of the stock belongs to 6,200 employees.

Ed Hinshaw started as an announcer for the *Journal*'s radio-TV station four decades ago. He eventually became a TV anchor and now is one of the company's top executives. Hinshaw says the stock plan "has had a dramatic impact on my own life and that of my family." He credits it with enabling him to own a boat, to travel, to educate his sons, and "to be confident of financial security for a long time to come. It has made an immense difference in an industry known for gnawing people and spitting their remains in the wind."

11. **Shorten the time that we work.** Between the late 19th century and the mid-20th century the workweek was reduced from 80 hours to 40 hours. But although we have had huge gains in technology, productivity, and population in succeeding decades, we have failed to come to grips with the implications of having too many people for the work that needs to be done, of having too few people doing too much of the work and others none at all, and of having a widespread feeling of pressure and

Shorter work time doesn't just mean a shorter workweek. It can also mean:

☞ Longer vacations (Sweden requires five weeks, for example).
☞ More job-sharing and other alternative employment arrangements.
☞ Better family leave policies. One business set up an inexpensive and effective cooperative day care program by giving time off in rotation to workers to run the program from their own homes.
☞ Less overtime.

alienation in a country that should be able to celebrate its plenty. As Peter Leyden has put it, "We may well need another New Deal . . . and this New Deal may not just redistribute money—it might also redistribute time, in the form of shorter workweeks for everyone."

Our concept of work is in no small part a product of the industrial counterrevolution of the late 19th century. Barbara Brandt of the Shorter Work-Time Group notes that "in pre-industrial (particularly hunting and gathering) societies, people generally spent 3 to 4 hours a day, 15 to 20 hours a week, doing the work necessary to maintain life." Today Americans work longer and take shorter vacations than in any industrialized country except Japan.

Brandt notes that we have developed a system that offers only two options: long work hours or unemployment. "Those lucky enough to get full-time jobs are bribed into docile compliance with the boss, while the specter of unemployment always looms as the ultimate punishment for the unruly."

A shorter workweek would have a considerable impact on jobs: The United Auto Workers estimated a few years ago that if overtime were eliminated, there would be 88,000 new jobs created in the auto industry alone. In Germany, instead of laying off workers, Volkswagen plants went on a 4-day 29-hour workweek. Jobs saved: 20,000. And the European metal workers' union estimates that 800,000 jobs were saved by cutting workweeks for their members.

12. **Buy from firms that do right; boycott those that don't.** Like every individual and other institution in America, businesses need ethics, values, and a sense of responsibility to their community. Nothing has been as corrupting to this country as the idea that the bottom line is the one and only commandment that need be followed. We can help change this by patronizing the businesses that are

trying, boycotting the ones that aren't, and looking for the words *Made in the USA.*

And now a final word from one of America's great businessmen

Peter Drucker, in an interview with *Wired* magazine, told of a financier who "gave an order to his investment people never to invest in a company in which a CEO earned more than 30% more than the next layer. That CEO, he said, can't build a team, and the company is mismanaged. He also once said that the proper ratio for salaries for employed people, between the top people and the rank & file, should be twenty-fold, post-tax. That's the highest. Beyond that, you create social tension." In fact, in 1995, the average Fortune 500 CEO was earning 157 times as much as a factory worker—up from 41 as much in 1960.

The radical businessman described by Drucker was J. P. Morgan, the megatycoon who died in 1913.

An American Parts List

166 hours a year for each American
to read a daily paper

450,000 volunteer rescue squad workers

1.8 milllion injuries a year caused by
falling or tripping

2 million farms (down from 7 million in 1935)

460 milllion bank credit cards

1.1 billion containers of beer and soft drinks
consumed annually in California

7. How to stay alive
A poker player's guide to the environment

Three things really worth worrying about

1. Population growth
2. Climatic instability*
3. Food

If that's too many things to worry about, then just worry about population growth. Dealing with overpopulation will have a huge effect on the other two problems.

How I learned risk assessment

I was a poker player long before I started paying attention to environmental problems. One of the things I learned while playing poker is that you can

---

*I've used *climatic instability* in place of *global warming* because the latter phrase has unfortunately led some people to think that the worst that will come out of ecological indifference is a bad sunburn or, alternatively, that a 30-inch blizzard proves there's nothing to worry about after all.

from time to time beat the odds—but don't count on it. That's why you won't find me in Atlantic City or Las Vegas.

The second thing I learned is that even when you do beat the odds, don't count on its happening again. There's a big difference between one good hand and a whole good night.

The third thing I learned is that you can from time to time beat the odds—but you usually have to stay in the game long enough for it to happen. Meanwhile, you can lose an awful lot of money. You have to calculate not only the odds but the stakes as well. And you are always on the edge.

Three scenes from the edge

1. A little girl makes a sand castle. It is a beautiful day and a beautiful sand castle, constructed not far from the edge of the water. The tide has risen only halfway. Then the girl's mother calls her for lunch. They go to a little carryout near the beach and do some shopping. When they finally return, it is high tide. The little girl looks for her castle, but the sea has come in and washed it all away. She is sad, but her mother says they can come back tomorrow and build another one.

   If the little girl had consulted an oceanographer (or even an older kid), she might have learned that the probability of her castle's being destroyed approached certainty and that she could have avoided catastrophe by moving the construction site to a safer, if less appealing, location.

   On the other hand, should she have been accosted by a conservative columnist, she might have been informed that since the water had been safely rising for four hours and thirty-three-minutes, it was clear that her castle was not in any danger. Anyone who told her otherwise was an antigrowth, knee-jerk liberal alarmist.

2. During their vacation the girl's mother rents a house right at the edge of the beach. It is a beautiful house next to a beautiful beach. It is constructed on stilts between the highway and the first line of dunes. The following winter the mother gets a call from the real estate agent saying that she'll have to choose another location for next summer; a gale has destroyed the house and several others near it.

> Calvin Trillin says that he didn't do well in math or science because he couldn't explain to his teachers that his answers were meant to be ironic.

The agent calls it a "freak storm"; the mother explains it to her child by saying it was an "accident."

In fact, such storms occur in this area every 7 years on average. Over the years some 32 houses have been destroyed or badly damaged just along this stretch of beach. The owners had worried a bit about the danger when they first built the house, but no one else seemed

AND SO DO SCIENTISTS . . .

Historians differ.

—Appalachian folk singer on being told after his rendition of "Bonaparte Crossing the Rockies" that Napoleon never visited America

concerned, so eventually they stopped thinking much about it. Besides, they read an article that said that "scientific support for the notion of a drastic rise in sea level has waned rapidly." The article didn't note that the Intergovernmental Panel on Climate Change had reported that over the past 100 years, sea levels had, in fact, risen 4 to 8 inches. Or that this was enough, according to the Environmental Defense Fund, "to have eroded over 40 feet of a typical barrier beach on the East Coast of the United States." Or that the *New York Times* reported that "At the most likely rate of rise, some experts say, most of the beaches on the East Coast of the United States [will] be gone in 25 years. They are already disappearing at an average of 2 to 3 feet a year."

3. At home or at the beach the little girl and her mother live on another edge. With nearly 6 billion other humans, they exist in that thin layer where the atmosphere and the earth's crust meet. Like many parents these days, the mother finds herself occasionally worrying about the world in which she is raising her daughter. She's confused. For example, there was a 1995 story

The leaky roof can fool the sun, but it can't fool the rain.
—Creole proverb

about global warming in the *Washington Post* that split the arguments so neatly one could easily reach the author's own conclusion: "When you sort through the confusion, how much you worry about greenhouse warming turns out not to be a matter of science." The story quoted a MIT professor: "It comes down to personality, it comes down to politics."

Then, just two months later, the *New York Times* reported: "In an important shift of scientific judgment, experts advising the world's governments on climate change are saying for the first time that human activity is a likely cause of the warming of the global atmosphere." When her daughter asks her a question about global warming, she doesn't know quite what to say.

What poker teaches us about life at the edge

The principles of poker, it turns out, are useful lessons for thinking about the environment as well. Let's return to the sand castle for a moment. There is a 100 percent probability that the little girl faces ecological disaster. The castle will definitely be washed away. On the other hand, she is only playing a penny ante game. In building the castle, she's engaged in a random act of harmless amusement. Her distress over her loss will be temporary; after all, she can build another one right away. Further, no one—and nothing—suffer permanent damage by either the castle's construction or destruction.

With the beach house, the game changes. The chances of destruction are far less but still objectively calculable. Mathematically minded homeowners could have figured what the chances were of losing their houses during a winter storm or, far more important, during all the winter storms that might occur in their lifetimes.

> ## FROM THE LAND OF SKY BLUE WATERS . . .
>
> Canadian health officials have told some Eskimo women not to breast-feed because of high levels of contaminants in their milk. Although the source is not known, the Arctic Ocean can preserve for 60 years contaminants that would disappear in a few hours in southern waters.

Incidentally, these two sets of odds are not the same. If you toss a coin, there is a 50 percent chance it will come up tails; if you repeatedly toss a coin, however, there is almost a 100 percent chance that it will eventually come up tails.

Now if the downside of your game is not merely a coin that lands tails up, but the loss of your house—or a nuclear plant radiation leak or a massive oil spill—then the probability of something's happening *ever* becomes far more important than the probability of its happening on a particular occasion.

Finally, we come to the ultimate game, a long future of uncertainty and highly disputable odds, in which the ante is the earth and human life itself. Here is the opposite of the sand castle problem; now we have unknown odds but enormous stakes.

> ## TWO BAD BETS
>
> 1. To assume that there is no risk until you prove there is a risk
> 2. To assume that there is no risk in doing nothing

So what does poker have to tell us?

It says you have to know when to hold them and know when to fold them. As a rule of thumb, whatever the odds, you don't want to bet either your house or your planet on a game of chance.

What the odds can't tell you

Oddsmakers assume a certain stability in the system for which they are making their projections. For example, the odds in poker assume no one is going

---

A POKER PLAYER'S GUIDE TO ENVIRONMENTAL RISK ASSESSMENT

1. Calculate the stakes as well as the odds.
2. The odds of something's happening at any moment are not the same as the odds of something's *ever* happening. In ecological calculations—especially ones in which the downside could ruin your whole millennium—it is the latter odds that are important.
3. When confronted with conflicting odds, ask what happens if each projection is wrong. Job loss because of environmental restrictions may come and go, but the loss of the ozone layer is something you can have forever.
4. When confronted with conflicting odds, remember that you don't *have* to play the game. There are other things to do with your time—or with the economy or with the environment—that may produce better results. Thus, instead of playing poker, you could be making love. Or instead of jobs deriving from some air- or water-degrading activity, the same jobs could come from more benign industry, such as retrofitting a whole city for solar energy.
5. Don't let anyone—in industry, government, or the media—define an "acceptable level of risk" for your own death or disease. Others may not have the same vested interest in the right answer as you do.
6. If the stakes are too high, the game is not worth it. If you can't stand the pain, don't attempt the gain.

---

to stand up with a pistol and peremptorily remove all the money on the table. The bookie assumes that the fifth at Pimlico will be run without his favorite horse's being doped. And so forth. Similarly, nature is in many ways a remarkably stable and resilient system and predictably capable of adjusting to changing conditions.

It is this characteristic, in fact, that leads some scientists to suggest that we may be unduly alarmed about our ecological future.

On the other hand, the fact that everyone, to some extent, is guessing suggests something in itself—namely, we don't have all the facts upon which to determine the odds. And if we don't have all the facts, we could be in for some enormous surprises.

Take the Gulf Stream, for example. We simply don't know what changes in climate or water currents and temperatures might cause the Gulf Stream to shift directions. As Stanford population studies professor Paul Ehrlich has pointed out, "what scares [experts] is the knowledge that weather is driven by small differences between large numbers."

Let's imagine, for example that some climatic change causes the Gulf Stream to cross an invisible threshold, and as a result it moves away from Europe. A very small but very wrong alteration could easily create the world's newest ski resorts in the hills of Wales, give Ireland the climate of Nova Scotia, and make London (at least until everyone moves out) the largest Arctic city in the world. Bear in mind that London sits near the latitude of Winnipeg, Nice and the Riviera are due east of Boston, and Paris lies north of Quebec.

We see the dramatic effect of small change every day when water turns to ice or snow or steam. Without a thermometer, we'd be hard pressed to know just when a tiny change in the temperature of our water would drastically alter its character. That's the problem we face in trying to figure what climate is up to. We are always living close to the edge.

We must also ask ourselves how many thresholds we have already silently and unknowingly passed. For example, Anne E. Platt, writing in Worldwatch's *Vital Signs 1995*, notes that the rate of breast cancer has increased around the world by 1 to 2 percent a year since 1930. The rate of prostate cancer has also been steadily rising. In America the chances of getting breast cancer has gone from 1 in 20 in 1960 to 1 in 8 today. Italy, Japan, Brazil, and China all have experienced a doubling in the prostate cancer rate between 1970 and 1985.

We don't know why this has happened. There is evidence, Platt points out, that breast cancer is affected by such factors as "age of

LOOKING IN THE RIGHT PLACE . . .

The popular media tend to discount environmental factors in writing health stories, putting the burden for prevention on their readers and their doctors. For example, searching through a computer database for magazine articles that contained the phrase *breast cancer*, I came up with 2,018 stories. Then I asked the computer for articles that contained the word *environment* as well as *breast cancer*. There were only 257 of them. Further, those articles that emphasized the potential role of chemicals and pollutants in breast cancer were typically found in scientific journals rather than in popular women's magazines. Take a look at the ads in the latter publications, and you may be able to guess why.

first menstruation, menopause, and first child; obesity and the intake of fiber and alcohol. Yet these factors combined account for only 20–30 percent of all cases of breast cancer." There is also evidence suggesting that lowering

Why saving the environment is a macho cause

A study of Scottish men found that those born after 1970 have sperm counts on average 24 percent lower than those born in 1968. The good news is that the sperm counts are not low enough to affect fertility. Yet. They will, however, become so if the decline continues into the next century.

The AP reported that "researchers say environmental estrogens are a prime suspect. These are chemicals that mimic the female sex hormone estrogen and are found in substances ranging from detergents to plastic wrappers."[x] Dr. Charles Tyler, a researcher at Brunel University, told the BBC that fish exposed to estrogens emerge with the characteristics of both sexes: "There is very strong evidence now to show that there are chemicals out in the environment which can affect sexual development. Certainly, in regard to the supermarket now, I try and buy goods which aren't well prepackaged so they don't use a lot of the chemicals which we have been researching."

The study backs up an earlier one that looked at 61 scientific papers from 1938 to 1991 and found a "remarkable change" in sperm count "probably due to an enviromental factor."

Among the suspected chemical components are phthalates. Here are a few of the things that contain phthalates: plastic, paints, inks, adhesives, detergents, herbicides, pesticides, cardboard used for food packaging, plumbing pipes, and paper. They also find their way into water. Says researcher John Sumpter: "You can't have a Western life of any sort at all without being exposed to phthalates."

And infertility is not the only problem. Dr. Theo Colborn, a senior scientist at the World Wildlife Fund, says the strongest evidence of chemicals' disrupting human life is to be found in studies on hyperactivity. Endocrine-disrupting chemicals may also be causing a decline in intelligence and short-term memory.

*Even more disturbing research suggests a synergistic effect when two or more of these environmental estrogens are combined, producing results many times more potent than when just one chemical is involved.

An incomplete list of really weird things happening in the nineties

The Midwest has two "100-year floods" in 3 years.

After 5 years without a substantial frost, New Orleans is overrun by cockroaches and termites.

Frog populations start dropping quickly in 140 countries.

The 10 hottest years ever recorded occur in a 15-year period.

Mountain glaciers retreat significantly all around the world.

Northeast Brazil gets hit with the worst drought in a century while Rio de Joneiro gets three times as much rain in just eight January days as it normally gets in the whole month.

London has the driest summer since 1727 and the hottest since 1659

A heat wave in the Midwest leaves 800 people dead

There are record levels of rain in western Australia. Meanwhile, eastern Australia has its first rainless August ever recorded.

There are 11 hurricanes in one season off the U.S. East Coast—the most in over 60 years.

The average surface temperature of the earth is the highest ever recorded.

The American East Coast has record-breaking snows while Alaska gets hardly any.

Finally, an iceberg the size of Rhode Island or Yosemite Park breaks off the Larsen Ice Shelf—the ponytail of Antarctica—where the average summer temperature has risen almost four degrees.

fat intake and exercising more reduce the chance of breast cancer. And of course there has been better detection of illness, and more people are living long enough to get the disease.

But there is also the possibility that the cancer is affected by "pollutants and chemicals that duplicate or interfere with the effects of estrogen." In fact, notes Platt, "breast cancer mortality in pre-menopausal Israeli women declined by 30 percent following regulations to reduce levels of DDT and carcinogenic pesticides in dietary fat."

Adding up the numbers

Often—as when building a sand castle on an incoming tide—you don't need the oddsmakers at all. You can just look it up. For example, on this page are some figures that are pretty solid: how many there are of us and how many there are going to be, given current trends and habits.

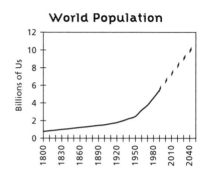

Here's another way of looking at it: We know it took about 4 million years for humans to populate the earth with its first billion humans. It took just 100 years for the second billion, 35 years for the third, 15 years for the fourth, and 12 for the fifth. The world is growing by 10,800 people an hour, adding the equivalent of a city the size of Newark, New Jersey, every day.

Former Wisconsin Senator Gaylord Nelson, counselor of the Wilderness Society, has a good way of looking at it. At the current rate of growth, he says, the population of the United States will double in less than 70 years. So at some point around the middle of the next century, we are likely to have (or need) twice as much of everything we have now. Twice as many cars, trucks, planes, airports, parking lots, streets, bridges, tunnels, freeways, houses, apartment buildings, grade schools, high schools, colleges, trade schools, hospitals, nursing homes, prisons.

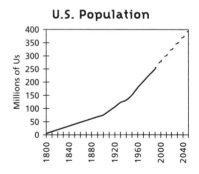

Imagine your city or town as it would look with twice as much of everything. Oh, yes, don't forget to add twice as much farmland, water, and food if you can find them. And twice as many chemicals and other pollutants in the air and water, twice as much heat radiation from all the new construction, twice as much crime, twice as many fires, twice as big traffic jams, and twice as many walls with graffiti on them.

Not that everyone accepts this scenario. There are those who think we can, with the help of science and technology, feed tens of billions more people. Some of them are scientists who admit that life will be degraded but think it still physically possible. Some are Roman Catholic bishops, who said a few years ago that the earth could support 40 billion people.

Some are the voices of industry or think tanks. Their argument is based on the economic notion that growth is an unmitigated virtue and that anything opposed to growth is wrong. Many of them are economists, who, as Amory Lovins has said, "are people who lie awake nights worrying about whether what actually works in the world could conceivably work in theory."

Gaylord Nelson suggests some questions for them: "Do the unlimited growth folks really believe that the more crowded the planet becomes, the freer and richer we will be? Do they think a finite planet with finite resources can sustain infinite economic expansion and population growth? If not, where do they draw the line? They don't say."

> Billions are hard to visualize. Journalist Tim Wiener once put it this way: One thousand seconds is about 17 minutes. One million seconds is about 11 1/2 days. One billion seconds is about 32 years.
>
> Financial analyst Stephen Todd uses a different scale: "A billion seconds ago Eisenhower was president. A billion minutes ago Christ was walking the earth. A billion hours ago people were living in caves."

The real problem with Wonder bread

Sooner or later discussions of the environment's future get around to talking about food. One of the great changes in America over the past 50 years has been the removal of most of us from the sources of our physical sustenance. Less than 2 percent of us live on a farm anymore.

It's easy for children to grow up today without a clear understanding of where those objects in the supermarket actually come from. When a supervisor at the Voice of America sent around a memo banning knives in employees' desks—"for the purpose of cutting bread and/or other food-related products"—she was unconsciously reflecting the degree to which we have come to see what we eat as a product—only vaguely related to a living source.

The real problem, however, with Wonder bread is not its manufacture or its artificial ingredients but that so much of it still must be grown. Since it

THINGS THAT SHOW WE ACTUALLY CAN DO SOMETHING ABOUT IT

In 1994 there were only 2 new starts on nuclear plants (both in China) and only 40 plants under construction. This was the lowest figure in a quarter century.

Global production of those chemicals that have been depleting the ozone layer has fallen dramatically since 1988.

The number of nuclear warheads has dropped 35 percent since 1986.

The great bald eagle has come off the endangered species list.

The amount of lead in gasoline in the Northern Hemisphere has dropped dramatically since 1970.

Wal-Mart is starting to build energy-efficient stores. These stores cost 10 percent more to build, but Wal-Mart expects a payback from utility savings in two to three years.

For the first time since they were measured, the total amount of ozone-destroying chemicals in the lower atmosphere declined in 1995.

THE ENVIRONMENT AS A NEWS BEAT

... far more important than Wall Street or Washington. Its laws are stronger than Newt's; its moves are more important than the Federal Reserve's. Its impact overwhelms that of the stock market or the next election. ...

The environment is not one player on the field. It is the field. It holds up, or fails to hold up, the whole economy and all of life, whether the spotlight is on it or not.

—Donella Meadows

---

must be grown in places like the great wheat fields of Iowa, those who project an unlimited future must assume, in the words of Paul Ehrlich in a talk to EPA staffers,

that we are going to turn all the arable land in the world into a simulation of Iowa, with the same climate as Iowa, and twenty-five Ph.D.s standing around every experimental hectare during the growing season. ... You also assume that none of the 40 billion people will stand on farmland, that the climate will remain the same, and that there will be no acid rain. With all these little assumptions, you might get a number like 40 billion or 60 billion. It depends on whether you assume you can farm the ocean surface, or grow corn underneath a Greenland ice cap.

How soon do we have to worry about running out of food? A 1986 study published in *Bioscience* estimated that humans were at that time co-opting about 40 percent of the world's food supply consumed by 30 million species. Even assuming that we didn't allow the other species another bite, on the basis of current supplies humans could multiply only by about 150 percent before the wheat, its foodlike products, and everything else gave out. We would then have mass starvation. Deaths not in the millions, as in the Holocaust, but in the tens of millions or hundreds of millions.

One more thing . . .

Even if there is enough food to go around, we may not really get to enjoy it that much. Bear in mind Dr. Calhoun's mice. Dr. John Calhoun was a scientist who put four pairs of white mice in a steel cage eight and half feet on a side. Within two years the mice had increased to 2,200, and it was not a pretty sight. The adult mice started excluding the young mice from their company, and the young began biting, attacking, and slashing one another. Finally social and sexual intercourse became impossible without the mice's being bashed. They stopped

Why saving the environment is a feminist cause

Global population efforts are deemphasizing birth control programs. Despite the obvious value of birth control and sex education, they often didn't work anywhere near well as planners hoped. What does seem to work, even though it's harder and slower, is raising the economic status of women. As women earn more and become economically and socially independent, they no longer feel the need for large families to support them.

reproducing. In time there was none to replace them, and eventually all the mice just died out.

How to keep people from laughing when you try to save the environment

Americans don't trust businesses to clean up the environment. One poll found over three quarters of the respondents agreeing that "business is only concerned with profits and not with the environment."

But here's the rub. The same poll found that nearly two thirds agreed with the statement that "environmentalists are usually too extreme."

Many environmentalists think they're doing the Lord's work. Many Americans think they're just practicing a peculiar religion.

In fact, Americans already worry about the environment; many do something about it. One of the best-kept secrets about Americans is how environmentally concerned we are. We express this concern through some 12,000 grass-roots groups with a membership of 14 million.

Americans, even those in the supposed heartlands of antienvironmentalism, overwhelmingly consider themselves supporters of the environment. A 1995 survey by the University of Idaho found that 76 percent of those polled in the Columbia River basin said protecting water, watersheds, ecosystems, wilderness, fish, wildlife, and endangered species habitats are the most important uses of the region's public lands. Only 23 percent thought logging, mining, and grazing were the most important.

And we're not dumb about these issues either. Nearly two thirds of Americans agree that it is probably or definitely true that when we use coal, oil, or gas, we contribute to the greenhouse effect. Over half consider solar energy the best power source for the enviroment. In 1994, 46 percent expressed a willingness to pay higher prices to protect the environment.

So why is there a widespread notion that Americans are deeply divided on ecological questions? Here are a few reasons:

In *Where We Stand,* the authors rank the United States against other countries by 1,000 standards. Here's how America ranked on a few environmental issues:

- Percent of all glass recycled: 14th out of 16 countries
- Percent of all paper and cardboard recyled: 13th out of 14
- Waste per person per year: 1st out of 19 (and more than twice as much as the Brits)
- Carbon dioxide (the greenhouse stuff) released per person per year: 1st out of 8 (and twice as much as Germany)
- Carbon monoxide (smog) released annually: 1st out of 13 (and more than the next 12 combined)
- Chemical and biological waste generated each year: 1st out of 20 (7 times as much as the next 19 combined)

- When we disagree on a particular environmental issue, the media tend to expand this conflict to environmental matters in general. Thus we may forget that even those not concerned about saving the spotted owl probably want to have clean air and water.
- We get our feelings toward the environment all mixed up with personal and cultural values. Environmentalists often see hunters as heartless killers; hunters often see environmentalists as hippie tree huggers. What should be a debate over ecology becomes one over culture, values, and lifestyles. There's a tendency to favor the environment but scoff at environmentalists.
- The media's view of the environment is skewed by the fact that their readers/viewers and their advertisers want different things. What is presented as a conflict between different groups of Americans may really be a conflict between the two markets for which the media contend: advertising and circulation. The former often wins out.

Some road signs

- ☑ Number of chemicals in commercial use today: 70,000. Number that have been tested for their health effects: less than 1 percent
- ☑ Number of different contaminants found in American drinking water: 1,000. Number for which the federal government has set concentration limits: 83.
- ☑ Typical reduction of visibility at the Grand Canyon caused by pollution: 50 percent or greater.
- ☑ Percent of oysters harvested in Chesapeake Bay compared with a century ago: 1 percent
- ☑ Number of tons of unwanted dead or dying fish and other marine life thrown back into the world's oceans every year: 18 million
- ☑ Percent of ozone depletion in the Antarctic: 60 percent
- ☑ Amount you would have to pay for gas if all hidden costs were included: $10 a gallon
- ☑ Number of new cities China plans to build in the next 15 years despite strict population control: 381

Here are a few ways to cut through the rhetorical smog that often hovers over environmental discussions:

- ☑ **Speak United States.** This rule, taught me by my high school math teacher, Mr. Breininger, was the best literary advice I ever got. Too often environmental issues are discussed in scientific, legal, or regulatory jargon. How are you going to win someone to your way of thinking about the Delaney Clause or salvage rights if they don't know what they are?
- ☑ **Get the lawyers under control.** The environmental movement, like much of public interest politics, derives a good deal of its tactics and strategies from lawyers. There is a bias toward regulatory approaches that keeps environmental and corporate lawyers front and center and leads to many bad compromises and solutions.

☑ **Include people in what you're saving.** Human beings are part of the environment too. Human starvation in Africa should be considered at least as important by environmentalists as what's happening to elephants. Urban neighborhoods should be considered human marshes as worthy of protection as any wetland. I like to use the word *ecology* instead of *environment* whenever possible because it stresses the interconnectedness of life. A lot of people think of the environment as something "out there," just a background that is separate from them.

☑ **Accept complexity and ambiguity.** Not every environmental issue is an open-and-shut case. For example, a forestry professor pointed out to me once that if it hadn't been for fox hunting, there probably wouldn't be any foxes left in England. I couldn't argue with him.

☑ **If you can avoid it, don't make people clean up after the polluters.** For example, the EPA passed regulations that required car owners in certain states to undergo a difficult emissions test. The inspection sites were to be few and far apart, and there was a high chance that owners would be hit with repair bills mounting into the hundreds of dollars. There were loud protests. People told the EPA it should make manufacturers build clean cars instead of making car owners bear the cost in a random and unpredictable fashion.

☑ **Get kids involved.** Kids often have a more natural feel for ecological issues than adults do. And they're effective advocates. I learned that from my oldest son, who, when he was in third grade, used to say, "Don't smoke, Dad," whenever I lit up my pipe. At the time I thought some fascist teacher was brainwashing him, but it got me to give up smoking.

The EPA eventually rescinded the regulations.

☑ **Don't try to do everything in Washington.** The federal 55 mph speed limit may have increased safety and reduced fuel consumption, but it undermined the 10th Amendment, annoyed a lot of people, reduced respect for the government, and contributed to the growth of the militia movement. If the issue had been handled at the state level, where it constitutionally belonged, many of these problems could have been avoided. To be sure, after repeal some states set higher speed limits than many environmentalists thought wise. But the ecology of American politics is better off. That's important too. Besides, the liberal bias against state and local action is often unfounded. In 1992, for example, the one hundred largest localities in America pursued an estimated 1,700 environmental crime prosecutions, more than twice the number of such cases brought by the federal government in the previous decade. Similarly, as Washington was vainly struggling to get a handle on the tobacco industry, 750 communities passed indoor no-smoking laws.

☑ **Don't be a prig.** Environmentalism lends itself to self-righteousness. This can be avoided by emphasizing a politics of enlightened self-interest rather than one of moral enlightenment. For example, many environmental issues are also public health issues. Treating them as such may help citizens grasp their meaning far better than emphasizing the damage being done to the atmosphere or to seemingly exotic species. Working closely with labor unions and ethnic groups, as well as developing a community consensus on ecological goals, can help turn people's environmental instincts into constructive action.

> Number of members of Congress who voted in 1995 against improved drinking water standards and then bought bottled water for their offices with tax dollars: 79

Herman Daley's healthy heresies for a sick planet

Herman Daley is a visionary economist who used to be with the World Bank and now teaches at the University of Maryland. Here are three ecological-oriented economic remedies he proposes:

- **Stop counting the use of natural resources as income.** When we use up natural resources, we are losing something, not gaining it.

- **Tax labor and income less; tax instead the flow of energy and materials coming from the earth (as natural resources) and returning to the earth (as waste).** Rather than tax what you want—income and profits—tax what you don't want—resource depletion and pollution.

- **Move away from free trade and toward developing internal markets.** Globalizing the economy means eroding much of the national government's ability to do things for the common good. Under global trade rules, any protection of local businesses, or of the environment, can be struck down as a restraint of trade. Trade is wrongly treated as the highest value, to which all other values must be sacrificed.

An American Parts List

35,000 square miles of paved & gravel roads—enough
to cover all of Indiana

65,000 vacant lots in Detroit

1 Barbie doll sold every second

3 million young people who volunteer their time

11,000 7-Eleven stores

927 microbreweries

8. How to enjoy the 'hood again
Designing urban places for those who actually live there

You think things are bad now?

Cities have always had problems. Neighborhoods of medieval Damascus, for example, were controlled by gangs that wore distinctive colors and specialized in robbery, looting, and assassination. Architectural critic Charles Lockwood quotes a mayor of New York City as declaring in 1839: "This city is infested by gangs of hardened wretches," who "patrol the streets making night hideous and insulting all who are not strong enough to defend themselves." And William Blake in the eighteenth-century poem, "London," evoked images of chimney sweeps—often children as young as six working naked in soot-lined towers—and of the syphilis being spread from prostitutes to customers to their wives and their babies.

Clearing out

One way to deal with urban problems is to clear out. Since 1970 one third of the population of Cleveland and Detroit has moved out without being replaced. Atlanta, D.C., Baltimore, and Philadelphia have each lost about 20 percent of their population, Chicago 17 percent. St. Louis has lost half its citizens since 1950.

But when we leave, where do we go? To another city or something barely distinguishable from it. Less than a quarter of us live in rural areas. And when we speak of the suburbs, we are increasingly only describing a different sort of urban location. We now choose between styles of urbanity, not between cities and something else.

Still, whatever one's complaints about urban America, only 4 U.S. metropolitan areas make it on to the list of 50 largest cities in the world. In fact, all but 3 U.S. cities (New York, Los Angeles, and Chicago) are below the maximum threshold of 2 million citizens, at which point some demographers believe it becomes much more difficult to maintain a decent standard of living.

A short, unhappy history of the American city

Although cities have always had countervailing virtues and faults—and have always been the center of a struggle between exploiters and the exploited—there is a current perception by many that our country's major cities are not worth the candle. This feeling didn't grow overnight or by accident. Here are a few things that happened to the American city along the way:

In the 1950s the liberal Supreme Court justice William O. Douglas wrote in defense of the country's first massive urban renewal project, which flattened hundreds of acres in Southwest Washington: "The experts concluded that if the community were to be healthy, if it were not to revert again to a blighted or slum area, as though possessed by a congenital disease, the area must be planned as a whole." Tens of thousands of people were evicted, as were 800 businesses, 80 percent of which never reopened. This story was to be repeated many times throughout the country.

- The streetcar and then the automobile destroyed the compact city in which people lived and worked within walking distance and where—even when people were segregated by race or class—the separation was often measured in blocks rather than in miles.
- New zoning laws enforced the notion that work and home should be separate and that neighborhoods should be homogeneous in character.

- Suburbanization gained momentum, with greatly increased reliance on the car. Husbands left their neighborhoods for employment, and wives stayed home, close to children and schools.

- Post–World War II housing needs caused a new wave of suburbanization, this time encouraged by federal and private housing loan policies strongly favoring outlying construction over older urban dwellings.

- In the wake of this boom, cities were involuntarily decimated—socially, physically and economically. Freeways stabbed urban neighborhoods, and businesses drifted outward, following their customers, many of whom were members of long-standing white ethnic communities.

- In their places, cities became the final destination of a vast migration of poor southern blacks responding to a vision of opportunity and change. Blacks were eventually followed by Latinos and other immigrant groups.

- City planners found ways for the suburbanites to use the old city's still-useful downtowns without having to pay for them. With freeways (and, in a few cases, subways), suburban day-trippers could get in and out of the city easily.

- Following the riots of the sixties, the cities became places to fear and avoid. Instead of the hopeful rhetoric of the war on poverty, a language of urban despair arose. Rather than repair the damage to our cities, it seemed easier to rebuild them someplace else. As early as 1972 articles began appearing such as the one in *Fortune* headlined: DOWNTOWN HAS FLED TO THE SUBURBS.

- Planners started designing suburban pseudocities to compete directly with the old urban core. These were huge, sterile office-retail conglomerations that, unlike the traditional city, lacked culture, serendipity, economic opportunity, or ethnic and class diversity. Often they even lacked sidewalks; you were meant to come only by car. Meanwhile, various urban renewal schemes, convention centers, and the like attempted to reclaim portions of the old city from the poor and from remaining small businesses.

- The cost of neglecting the old cities soared in the 1980s with the war on drugs, Reaganomics, and cutbacks in urban aid. The cities now became places to occupy and control rather than to encourage and improve.

- In the end the commercial advantage of cities was eroded by the exodus of business, the community advantage by the new suburbs, the communications advantage by technology, the human advantage by cruel or indifferent policies, and the cultural advantage by television, film, and videotape. Increasingly Americans came to see those who still needed the cities—particularly the new immigrant and the unassimilated native poor—as threats to the common good, endangering their lives and wasting their tax dollars.

Edifice economics

The urban political response to all this was not to deal with the social implications or to meet imaginatively the economic challenge of the new suburbs. It was rather to change the look of the place, to find sweeping physical solutions to deeply human problems.

The idea, Richard Sennett has written, goes back to the 1860s design for Paris by Baron Haussmann, who, Sennett suggests, bequeathed us the notion that we could alter social patterns by changing the physical landscape. This notion was not

about urban amenities, such as park benches and gas lighting, or about technological improvements, such as indoor plumbing, but about what G. K. Chesterton called the huge modern heresy of "altering the human soul to fit its conditions, instead of altering human conditions to fit the human soul."

Eventually this idea produced waves of urban renewal, freeways, convention centers, stadiums, subways, pedestrian malls, aquariums, waterfront developments, and, most recently, proposals for casino and riverboat gambling—all in the name of urban progress and a happier tax base. But as one city's weekly paper asked about a planned aquarium, "How many big fish can the American public be expected to look at?" Few of these schemes would ever come close to realizing the claims made on their behalf. Few were little more than a

false front on a city's declining core and fraying soul.

Urban myths

Every self-respecting metropolis has a city magazine depicting the most mundane commercial activities with adjectival abandon. A style of business writing has arisen that transforms avaricious real estate developers into characters from a Raymond Chandler novel, whose every deal involves the mystery and tension of an international crisis. Meanwhile, architectural critics ascribe to the latest high-rise the grace of a Flemish oil.

This literature even fawns over the banalities of suburbia, producing such absurdities as author Joel Garreau's claim that suburban "edge cities" are "the most purposeful attempt Americans have made since the days of the Founding Fathers . . . to create something like a new Eden."

The idea that God's work has finally been successfully replicated by suburban real estate developers is challenged by the lives of ordinary citizens, most of whom think in terms of jobs, friends, and communities rather than of "contextual spaces" or regional markets. It also is markedly out of sync with the more personal literature of urban experience, ranging from Theodore Dreiser to Ice-T. Or with the stories we tell one another. A mother stuck in traffic five miles from a soon closing day care center would be hard pressed to feel the liberating benefits for women claimed for the new suburban utopia, and the unemployed inner-city dweller gets to enjoy few of the benefits of metropolitan growth his morning paper so enthusiastically describes.

Usually the goals of urban policy closely parallel the economic interests not of typical residents but of large corporations and the media organizations that serve them. These interests are not limited to the urban core but increasingly reach deep into the suburbs. While the wonders of metropolitan regionalism may produce a near-orgasmic response from a big-city newspaper editor, urban planning professor, or corporate executive, I have run into few other persons excited by the thought of living in a "region." Many, I suspect share the view of the character played by Michael Keaton, who in the movie *The Paper* screams at the globalist gray-haired *New York Times*ish editor, "I don't fuckin' live in the fuckin' world! I live in fuckin' New York City!"

Urban policies that don't work the way they're supposed to

Policy	What really happens
FREEWAYS	Although sold as transportation, these are primarily land development schemes making it easy for suburbanites to get into city jobs and for developers to get into new projects. Small businesses and neighborhoods are inevitably disrupted or damaged.
CONVENTION CENTERS, ARENAS, STADIUMS, AQUARIUMS	If properly planned, these can be of mild benefit to a city, but usually they are grossly overrated. Smith College Economics Professor Andrew Zimbalist estimates the benefits of a new sports franchise to be roughly the same as opening a branch of Macy's. Potential benefits are often dissipated by the wrong location, excessive city subsidy, cost overruns, faulty projections, and just plain corruption.
ENTERPRISE ZONES & OTHER CORPORATE INDUCEMENTS	These have generally been ineffective (except for corporate beneficiaries), all the more so because cities rarely write in enough protections for themselves. Programs are heavily weighted to help corporations rather than citizens.
REZONING	The modern equivalent of the king's grant of land to the nobility. Basically a gift of money by the city in the form of marketable air.
SPECIAL TAXES & TAX DISTRICTS	As more traditional schemes become unfeasible or too expensive, special taxes and tax districts begin cropping up. These tend either to give protected status to a pet political project or to force some taxpayers into subsidizing others.
COMPREHENSIVE PLANNING	When all else fails, announce that there'll be a new plan. It's a nifty way to help major commercial interests. The process is so complex and huge that citizens have a hard time getting a handle on what's really happening until it is too late.
SWEETHEART DEALS	The meat and potatoes of urban politics. Typically, major developers and commercial interests are wired closely to city hall. They know not only what to expect but where to expect it. A little advance knowledge can be worth millions yet often only costs a few thousands in campaign contributions.

Policy	What really happens
SPOT ZONING	Although city planners express deep respect for zoning, they have come up with a variety of ways—such as the planned unit development—to get around it. The result is called spot zoning. A PUD is essentially a rezoning of a specific site granted to a developer or group of developers. No ordinary homeowner has ever been granted a PUD.
PRIVATIZATION	Corrupt politicians used to sell city hall; now they give it away—and call it privatization.

The paradox of community

Although the word *community* is usually used in a positive sense, Americans' relationship with community has always been exceedingly ambivalent. This country was founded, and continues to be enriched, by those coming from distant communities that were oppressive, fossilized, or without economic opportunity. Yet as early as the 18th century the historian Gordon Wood points out, young men were leaving the new communities of their parents in New England to seek something still better farther west. We quickly came to associate freedom—and being an American—with mobility.

But then, as these Americans restlessly migrated west, they created countless fresh places. Not infrequently faith in community reincarnation was proclaimed by a name beginning with the word *New*. We ran away from community and built it at the same time. As the geographer Yi-Fu Tuan puts it, "Human lives are a dialectical movement between shelter and venture, attachment and freedom."

There are other paradoxes. For example, communities are perhaps easiest to build in times of stress or out of painful need. Impressive self-sufficient communities were constructed in New York's Harlem and Washington's Shaw in response to racial exclusion. These communities in many ways put their present counterparts to shame. Similarly, to many war veterans, few contemporary communities can compete with the bonds created under fire. Yet wistful as such memories may be, few would really attempt to recover them by reviving segregation or going back to war.

At other times, such as those of expansion, community may not seem important at all. The 18th-century trapper, the 19th-century western outlaw, and the 20th-century Wall Street buccaneer all considered themselves beyond community. And elites, such as academics, policy pushers, and journalists, tend to treat the theory and practice of communities other than their own as quaint and peripheral to larger concerns. (An exception, theoretically, is the political tribe known as communitarians. But their purpose seems more devoted to regulating than to creating communities.)

Community, and the desire for it, intrude even when our minds are supposed to be on something else. A report on violence in New York City's Washington Heights, for example, quotes a language teacher who says that among her students are gypsy cabdrivers and domestic workers who often work 15 hours before class and are too tired to learn much English. Why do they bother to attend? Explains the teacher: "To them it was a form of community and they participated to get that form of community."

It's not really that surprising when one considers that most large-scale social organization is but a century or so old. Urban sociologist Claude S. Fisher points out that "our species has lived in permanent settlements of any kind for only the last two percent of its history." As late as the 1850s, just 2 percent of the world's population lived in cities of more than 100,000, by 1900 only about 10 percent. By the end of the century about half the world's humans will live in cities.

But, notes ecological planner Ernest Callenbach, "we are medium-sized animals who naturally live in small groups—perhaps 20 or so—as opposed to bees or antelopes who live in very large groups. When managers or generals or architects force us into large groups, we speedily try to break them down into sub-units of comfortable size."

In short, what seems peripheral to some is probably really central; it may even be buried in our genetic code. Certainly, much of what we have come to think of as normal—the huge city, the massive state university, the megacorporation, the rock concert—is, in a historical and biological sense, not natural at all but rather human community on steroids.

The form of community also changes over time. Those who bowl alone these days—to use one sociologist's melancholic metaphor—may be doing so in part because their peers are over at the health club. Further, contemporary communities are often ones of belief, affinity, or habit more than of place. The places remain—the center city church, the gay district, the softball field of weekend dreams—but Americans today are as likely to commute to such communities as they are to live near them.

Nonetheless the business of fleeing bad, and building good, small communities, with all its concomitant excitement, success, failure, and ambivalence, remains key to our lives and our souls. Disappointing as it may seem to the producers and participants, MTV's *Real World* is actually a very old American story, the story of strangers in a new place making that place theirs. Together.

How to plan for everyone

COME UP WITH A PLAN.

It is a little-known fact that you don't need a license to plan your city or community. In fact, the sooner and better you do it, the less likely it is that someone else will do it for you. Every neighborhood, town, and city should have a citizen-drafted plan to compare with—or, better yet, replace—the official one. Here are some things to keep in mind as you get started:

- **Get everyone involved.** Keep the planning open and welcoming. Plan for everyone and with everyone. Don't just use the best-known local civic organizations. Even elementary schoolchildren can help plan a community; you can put their ideas up in store windows to get adults thinking as well. Seniors and the disabled have perspectives that are easily ignored. And asking alienated adolescents what they would like is a lot smarter than finding out later what they don't.
- **Find your own experts.** Architects, economists, anthropologists, public health workers, historians, and others can be a big help. Need a bike path? Ask the local bicyclists' association to give you a hand. Architects know how to talk the jargon of the zoning board; friendly economists can punch holes in the projections of city politicians. But beware of the planning and process hustlers and people with their own agendas. One way you can guess who these are is that they often use a lot of jargon and abstractions and already seem to have a plan. Use only experts you can understand.
- **Do a community inventory and biography.** Before discussing what you want, find out what you have. Don't try to imitate a conventional city

plan with its emphasis on physical form. Instead tell the community's story—where it has been, what it is, what it has and doesn't have, and what it would like to be. Describe its history, ecology, the people and places that help it function, unusual resources, major problems, neighborhood symbols, and community conflicts. Interview older residents and find out what the community has lost and gained in recent decades. Ask people why they live in your community, what they value about their places. Count things: number of seniors needing assistance, number of kids, parking spaces per shop, fires, burglaries. Find spaces in churches, schools, and other facilities that could be used for community purposes. Open spaces that could become pocket parks or urban gardens. Buildings that could be put to better uses. Identify neighborhood symbols and monuments.* Use your imagination. There is no one right way of doing it.

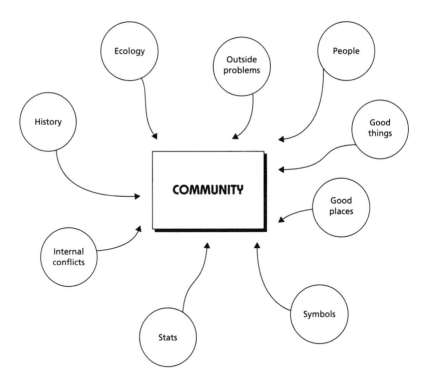

*A nickname for one urban neighborhood is the Big Chair—after a huge straight-back seat that once was a promotional icon for a long-departed furniture store.

GET GOOD STATS.

In Seattle and elsewhere people have started compiling indicators to help figure out how their communities are getting on. Some of these, such as the crime rate, unemployment, and air quality, are obvious, but Seattle also uses other data for its 40 indicators, such as the salmon count, volunteer involvement in the schools, and gardening activity. The work has not only affected city planning but influenced the name of the new comprehensive plan: Towards a Sustainable Seattle.

Such information can be a big help in public debates over city policy. One of the best places to discover these data is the government itself because it then becomes hard for city planners or politicians to refute it. For example, find out the budget of your local library, police station, and school. Then compare these figures with the total city budget for the appropriate departments. Are you getting your fair share? Is too much going for bureaucratic overhead? Such information should be generally known but rarely is.

CREATE NEIGHBORHOOD GOVERNMENT.

We can't rebuild our cities without rebuilding their neighborhoods, and we can't do that while denying these communities power and money. One way to shift the power in a city quickly and dramatically away from city hall is to create elected neighborhood councils with real powers: These powers should include:

- The right to incorporate
- The right to run community programs and businesses
- The right to provide city services under contract, including running local schools
- The right to have some measure of budgetary authority over city expenditures within their boundaries
- The right to have an important role in the justice system
- The right to sue the city government

Budgetary authority (not the actual money) could be granted over 1 percent of a community's pro rata share of a city's budget. Figure out what your neighborhood's share of 1 percent of the city's budget would be. I think you'll be surprised.

Changing How Planning Is Done

How planning has traditionally been done	How it could be done
Plan emphasizes major new building and destruction of old landscape. Plan assumes significant physical changes.	Plan emphasizes renovation and restoration of existing buildings and landscape. Plan assumes preservation of physical and social character that brought people to the community in the first place.
Planner's vision takes precedence over the community's values and desires.	Plan reinforces community values, desires, and social organization.
Citizens are seen as a problem: dysfunctional, "at risk," "permanent underclass."	Citizens are seen as an asset, sources of talent and ideas.
Plans and buildings dictate civic life.	Existing civic life determines nature of plans and use of buildings.
Plan implicitly presumes importing a "better class" of people. Code phrases include improved tax base and return of the middle class.	Plan is designed for people already living in the area.
Plan aims at meeting goals of largest businesses. Small businesses are often evicted to make way for new projects.	Plan emphasizes central role of small businesses.
Community remains primarily an importer of goods and services, economically dependent.	Community develops goods and services to export or use itself. Emphasis is on economic self-sufficiency.
Money coming into the community flows out again quickly.	Money coming into the community is recirculated, using community-based commercial and financial institutions, such as credit unions and cooperatives.
Outward physical order conceals inner social disintegration and alienation.	Anarchistic, jumbled, or even decaying facade conceals a well-functioning and complex social system.
Plan fights or exploits nature, adding to ecological disequilibrium.	Plan works with nature, seeking to mitigate past damage, create green solutions, and restore ecological equilibrium.
Plan emphasizes mobility—moving people considerable distances for work, services, shopping entertainment, and recreation.	Plan emphasizes access—keeping things people want and need as close as possible.
Plan relies on numbers, dollars, and aggregated phenomena.	Plan relies on individual experiences, stories, mutual hopes, and dreams.
Plan is skewed heavily toward presumed economic results. Social and cultural consequences are downplayed or ignored.	Plan has a holistic design, including everything from the economy to the environment and from cutting crime to embellishing culture.
Experts are outsiders selected by the city government.	Experts come from, or are selected by, the community itself.
To the average citizen, the plan is boring and difficult to understand.	To the average citizen, the plan is exciting and eazy to understand.

While one community might choose to spend its money on education, another might want more police patrols or recreation facilities. There would be mistakes, but they would be our mistakes and small mistakes, easier to understand and to rectify. Further, by permitting error, we would be permitting genius.

Neighborhood government is not some utopian scheme but a pragmatic approach. It is in fact contemporary large city government that is utopian in that there is no empirical evidence that it works well. It is under this form of government that we generally find the worst crime, the worst education, the worst health, the worst pollution, and the highest unemployment.

When developers announced plans for a neotraditional "village" named Frijoles near Santa Fe a few years ago, Olivia Tsosie wrote in *New Mexico Designer/Builder* about the difference between a true village and the proposed project: "A village is an autonomous social unit, with a reason for existing where it is. . . . What is a suburb? A dependent social unit with no internal reason for its existence. . . . Frijoles lacks work, resources, kinship, political or religious independence, and cohesion. . . . A village is a not-for-profit, organic, open-ended, human-scale social event, which becomes visible in its buildings and pathways."

END ECONOMIC BUSING.

Jane Jacobs in her *Cities and the Wealth of Nations* argues that "economic life develops by grace of innovating; it expands by grace of import-replacing." In other words, invent a better mousetrap and make your own cheese to go in it.

The idea of the city as a trading center goes back at least to ancient Greece. It is as applicable to L.A. or Chicago as it was then. Consider, for example, zip code 20032, one of the poorest in Washington, D.C. The neighborhood with zip code 20032 has a per capita income of $9,039. By American standards that's not much, yet the total household income of this one poor neighborhood is $370 million a year. What happens to that $370 million after it gets to the neighborhood is vital to what happens to the people who earn it. At present, much of the $370 million simply flows through the community and toward businesses, landlords, and financial institutions outside the neighborhood.

NEIGHBORHOOD FAIRNESS

One way to ease interneighborhood tensions over where public facilities should be located would be a neighborhood equalization board with power to make adjustments in where city funds are spent and where less desirable facilities are built. For example, if all the wards in a city save one have halfway houses, the commission might order the next facility to be built in the last ward, giving community groups there plenty of time to come up with specific locations. As it stands, we have elaborate protections and procedures to deal with discrimination against individuals, but few to handle discrimination in favor of or against whole communities.

A key to the economic revival of the older city is the development of self-generating economies. The self-generating economy has a long history in America. Many of the country's early communities were largely self-sufficient. This self-sufficiency, however, disappeared with the rise of the modern corporation. Capital began to flow through, rather than within, communities.

One can still, however, find self-generating urban economies although we seldom recognize them as such. The explosion of the legal profession, for example, reflects in no small part the ability of lawyers to create jobs for each other. And the yuppie phenomenon involves yuppies creating artificial needs for other yuppies, with some selling and others buying items that fulfill these needs.

The importance of such economies tends to be disregarded because they don't have the visible form of a single corporation or factory. Yet the impact can be dramatic. For example, if Washington's cabdrivers all worked for one company, it would be the largest private firm in the city.

Often citizens gang up on economic self-sufficiency because they find it isn't neat and orderly enough. Street vendors annoy local businesses; pedestrians complain about bike couriers; residents near universities hate group housing; others don't like gay bars; the local paper editorializes against gypsy cabs; others complain about illegal basement apartments or someone running a business out of her house. In my town even Christianity was declared disorderly as neighbors and bureaucrats teamed up to block a church that was feeding the poor.

What gets forgotten is that a city is not a private club. A city is a place used by large numbers of people for enormously disparate purposes. For many, the city is a means of upward mobility, and to the extent that it functions in this manner, this helps everyone. On the other hand, once you start defining people or their activities as socially unacceptable, you also start eliminating methods of survival and sources of public revenues.

We must recognize that at the heart of a city's material success is the balance of trade and self-sufficiency of that city's economy. Central to this, as Jacobs argues, is the replacement of imports. And central to this is small business. Not only has small business been the country's major producer of new jobs, but micro businesses—those with fewer than 20 employees—provided nearly half the new jobs between 1984 and 1990. Small business is more likely to hold on to its jobs, less often damaging to the environment, and less physically harmful to its workers.

THE ECONOMICALLY HEALTHY CITY

1. Makes things that other places need.
2. Makes a lot of the things that it needs.
3. Has places where these things can be made, including factories.
4. Strongly supports small business.
5. Doesn't overregulate entry-level jobs such as taxi driving or street vending.
6. Doesn't overregulate home business or prohibit small nondisruptive businesses in or near residential communities.
7. Does not overdevelop downtown so there are no places special shops and services can afford to rent.
8. Uses local financial institutions, such as credit unions, community banks, and lending circles, to keep money circulating within the community.
9. Has business leadership that is loyal to the city rather than to the metropolitan region.

Instead of helping small business, however, city legislators are prone to write regulatory measures with only big firms in mind, ignoring the effects their actions will have on a mom-and-pop operation. For example, over the past few years my town has lost thousands of jobs through the simple expedient of overregulating (or overenforcement of the laws regarding) street vendors, cabs, artist studios, street performers, interior decorators, and home occupations.

The taxi industry is an example of how cities often hurt themselves by restrictive policies. A study by the U.S. Department of Justice found that 87 percent of 100 cities with taxi service restricted entry in some way. Chip Mellor of the Institute for Justice has noted that Denver routinely turned down every application for a new taxicab company from 1947 on. Chicago and L.A. are closed. Boston's permit costs $60,000, and New York's $140,000. Washington, D.C., has been a rare case of free entry. The result: some 7,000 to 8,000 taxis in a city of fewer than 600,000. D.C. has 1 cab for every 75 citizens; NYC has 1 for every 600.

In 1994 Indianapolis eliminated the cap on taxi licenses, setting only maximum, but no minimum, fares. In four months the number of cab companies doubled, fares dropped 7 percent, and cabdrivers even started wearing ties.

One council member even went so far as to propose limiting where one could find live entertainment in bars. I don't think he was so much against music as he was inclined to think that unregulated human existence was intrinsically hazardous to health and morals. In this spirit the same politician also proposed the regulation of sperm banks—even though the city didn't have one.

One city's problem, however, can be another's moneymaker. For example, both Halifax and St. John in Canada hold successful weeklong festivals featuring street musicians from all over the world. Too often, though, it seems that every time someone thinks of a good way to make money outside of working for a major corporation, a city official comes up with a law to make it as difficult as possible. The result is a reduction in employment, more "illegal" activity, and a growing tendency toward concentration in the particular industry involved, since only the most powerful are equipped to deal with the regulatory morass. In fact, new restrictions on street vending cost my city 3,000 jobs at a time when everyone was talking about the need for new employment. In such ways the economic space between being homeless and being a junior partner is slowly emptied.

REJOIN THE CROWD.

Challenging the stereotype that urban density produces diminished quality, one study has found that per capita energy use in a high-density city is half that in a low-density city. Reasons include shared walls, increased use of bikes, easier access to public transit, shorter distances for sewage, gas, and water lines, and less energy to pump through them.

> A city is composed of different kinds of men; similar people cannot bring a city into existence.
>
> —Aristotle, *Politics*

Rebuilding a more compact community can occur in the most run-down neighborhood or in the most bland suburb. Architect Peter Calthorpe, for example, has designed "pedestrian pockets," which he describes like this: "A balanced, mixed-use area within a 1/4 mile walking radius of a light rail station. The uses within the zone would include housing, offices, retail, daycare, recreation and open space. Up to 2,000 units of housing and one million square feet of office can be located within three blocks of the light rail station using typical condominium densities and four-story office configurations."

Psychologists have found that it is the perception of crowding rather than actual density that really bothers people. Noise, traffic, and lack of open space can create claustrophobia even in low-density areas, while one can feel uncrowded in the pleasant densities you find, say, in San Francisco or in many European cities.

ALLOW CITIES TO MAKE MONEY.

We permit cities to own heavily subsidized mass transit but not income-producing land. This symbolizes the trap cities are in: They are not meant to lose money, but at the same time they are not allowed to make any. Yet cities always and everywhere have been a blend of the public and private. We should always be looking for good ways for our cities to make money. For example, land acquired by a city around important transit stops or for renewal projects could be leased rather than sold. Not only would the city get much more revenue this way, it could maintain better control over the use to which the land is put. Cities could own their own bank or credit unions, which could make loans to currently redlined neighborhoods and otherwise fill gaps left by private institutions.

REFORM ZONING

You may never have thought of getting a zoning change so you could build a high-rise office building where your house is now. Well, this is one of the ways that you are different from the typical developer. Developers make a lot of money out of what happens when land is rezoned. The difference in the value of the land before and after rezoning can be enormous.

In order to convince the city that this is a good idea, the developer hires lawyers and analysts who make arguments like: "It is economically unfeasible to build on this site under current zoning." This is a dumb argument since a plot of land can't be worth more than it's worth—unless, of course, you plan to change the zoning and make it worth more.

Everyone engaged in the politics of development knows that zoning can be changed. Thus the price of the land reflects what is going to happen once the planners come up with their justifications, the politicians receive their contributions or payoffs, and the newspaper editorializes in favor of the up-zoning. If, on the other hand, developers knew the zoning couldn't be changed, property values would quickly fall to a level commensurate with current zoning.

When government upgrades zoning, or exempts a parcel from some of its restrictions, it is giving away public property as much as if it handed out town recreation and park land free to corporations. That we cannot see and feel what has been given away may mislead us, but there is little doubt that the real estate developers know what it is and what it is potentially worth.

Rezoning is nothing less than an arbitrary license to make money while others are prohibited from doing so. In fact, this license can only be arbitrary. If everyone could get his or her lot rezoned to permit the construction of high-rise office buildings, the value of such rezonings would soon disappear with the saturation of the market.

Those who play this game don't even have to use their own money. One of the go-go speculators of the 1980s raised more than $300 million from 30,000 investors, the bulk of it used to invest in 6,000 acres of raw land outside Los Angeles, Phoenix, and Sacramento pending rezoning. Since Earth Day 1970 this country has lost more than 40 million acres of farmland to development, usually after local governments have rezoned the property for more intensive use.

Seven things wrong with zoning laws

1. Only the wealthy and the powerful get to change them.
2. The ease with which they are able to do this creates a speculative market in land.
3. Rezoning is a gift from the taxpayer to that small number of people who benefit from it. Although the size of the gift shows up in no account book, it can be worth millions of dollars.
4. Zoning laws separate our homes from our work. They also separate us by class, age, and race.
5. Zoning laws were premised on cheap auto fuel and the idea that all we needed to do with pollution was to move it some place else.
6. Zoning laws ignore the changed status of women. There has been no serious attempt to redesign cities in light of this change.
7. Zoning policies are important redistributors of wealth, but almost always in the wrong direction.

A few communities have tried to buck the trend. For example, in 1979 Seattle area voters approved a $50 million bond issue to pay farmers *not* to develop. Some 13,000 acres have been saved under this program.

Zoning laws were created early this century before we understood the ecological costs of a highway-dependent society and at a time when women were expected to stay at home. These conditions have changed but our zoning laws have not kept pace. For example, in homogeneous single-family, double-income neighborhoods whole blocks may now be deserted during the day, an invitation to crime. We spend our Saturdays driving to distant malls in part because we have zoned shops and services out of our own communities. While most communities would want to retain some form of zoning, this early-20th-century invention is long overdue for serious reform.

FIND PLACES FOR FOLKS TO LIVE.

Not everyone who leaves the city wants to. In a large number of cases, the cost and availability of housing provide the impetus. Among the factors that have raised the cost and lowered the availability has been gentrification. The gentrifiers not only upscale the housing stock but reduce it, since they require more space per capita in which to live than did former residents. Here are some ways we can find more living space in our cities:

Granny flats: One of the simplest, cheapest, and quickest ways is to permit people to add one apartment to their homes (called accessory apartments, granny flats, or mother-in-law apartments). Many of these apartments already exist illegally; there are an estimated 40,000 in L.A. alone.* The advantages of such apartments include lowering net costs for the homeowner, increasing the supply of housing, providing a social and economic mix within neighborhoods, allowing individual care to replace some social services (e.g., the young apartment dweller helping the aged landlord upstairs), providing neighborhood-based economic opportunity, and increasing the number of eyes on the street.

Boarders: Reviving the practice of taking in boarders could also greatly improve the availability of housing. The tradition of boarders and boarding-houses played a major role in the growth of the American city, providing newcomers with inexpensive places to stay and adding a source of income to those who had lived in the city long enough to buy houses. Like granny flats, the possibility has often been zoned out of existence or made excessively difficult.

Cohousing: Cohousing consists of individual homes clustered around a large common house with such facilities as a dining room, a children's playroom, a central kitchen, workshops, and laundries. The houses typically have their own small kitchens and are otherwise minimally self-sufficient but with an emphasis on communal facilities. Each cohousing plan is

---

*One of the best places to look for new ideas is in the underground economy. If normally law-abiding people insist on doing something against the rules, there's a good chance that they are on to something.

worked out with intense participation by future occupants. There is no single plan for these projects; they are designed for specific and changing needs and are hospitable to spontaneity. The cohousing approach has been used for condominiums, cooperatives and nonprofit rental housing.

Multifamily and growable homes: We could encourage the construction of more two- and three-family houses which were once a staple of urban America. We could build "grow houses" such as the 600-square-foot expandable designs of New Haven architect Melanie Taylor, which borrow from the compact plans of yacht interiors.

Mixed retail and residential construction: The classic combination of shops on the first floor and low-rise apartments above has virtually disappeared from the modern planners' repertoire even though it is one of the best ways to provide both commercial and residential space at reasonable cost.

NEED THE YOUNG.

It is commonly said that one needs a good education in order to get a good job. But it is also true that in order to have good schools, one needs good jobs. Educational systems rise and fall in response to the economy they serve.

A dramatic example occurred at the beginning of World War II. During the Depression years there was an assumption that many of the jobless were either too dumb or too lazy to find employment. After Pearl Harbor, however, such assumptions collapsed. America needed everyone, and in schools, factories, and the military the allegedly uneducable suddenly were able to learn.

Today there is an assumption that many of the urban jobless are either too dumb or too lazy to find employment. But unlike during World War II, this assumption is not being tested because we simply don't need everyone anymore. Instead we have let the social triage of race and class take its course.

To be sure, there are plenty of overbureaucratized, unimaginative, and just plain incompetent city school systems, but reforming them would be infinitely easier if students, administrators, teachers, and parents knew there was going to be an economic payoff at the end. When 50 percent of a city's welfare recipients have high school diplomas, there is a strong hint that something other than just the educational system is very wrong. Further, the word gets around. Politicians and the media may have abstract fantasies about the value of education; kids tend to be a bit more realistic.

So the most important first step toward a better urban school system is a better urban economy. The second step is to stop treating our young as an accident or crime waiting to happen and to begin respecting, helping, and needing them. We could, for example, use older students more as tutors and teachers of younger kids. We could use high schoolers as community organizers.

We could even teach students to become emergency medical technicians and community social service aides. Imagine if every urban high school had an emergency squad that not only was medically trained but was able to provide assistance to the elderly and infirm of the community and help staff clinics, schools, and recreation centers. With a classy uniform, good training, and equipment (along with a few perks like being on call on a rotating basis during the class day), schools and communities might find themselves with some impressive new role models. Can't be done? Well, it has been. On one Indian reservation a high school developed its own search and rescue squad, which has become a well-regarded part of the area's emergency services.

Test your local schools

Here are a few questions that may help you find out whether your schools are helping their students or just holding them. Add or subtract points for any statement that is true:

1. The principal
is seen regularly in classes finding out what's going on . . . .+10
is seen regularly in hallways in conversation with students . . . .+5
is seldom in the hallways but often on the PA system . . . .–5
uses a bullhorn in hallways . . . .–10

2. The school
has fewer than 500 students . . . .+10
has more than 500 students . . . .–5
is still trying to figure out this year's actual enrollment . . . .–10

3. The worst teacher in the school
just started this year 0

has been in the system 20 years . . . .–5

has just been named a downtown administrator . . . .–10

4. Older students are typically considered
potential teachers and tutors for younger students . . . .+10

members of a community . . . .+5

discipline problems . . . .–10

5. In history and social studies classes
students don't use textbooks because the teachers prefer regular books and
primary sources . . . .+10

students don't use textbooks because the system ran out and the new order
hasn't come in . . . .–5

What history and social studies classes? They were replaced by antidrug
programs a couple of years ago . . . .–10

6. Parents are
regularly used as volunteers in high school . . . .+10

regularly used as volunteers in elementary school . . . .+5

required upon coming to the school to sign a log and explain the purpose of
their visit . . . .–5

7. TV is used to
teach critical thinking about the media and advertising . . . .+10

make the curriculum more informative and interesting . . . .+5

view purple dinosaurs and show business kids from hell . . . .–5

8. Deduct 1 point for every TV commerical seen during the
typical school day. . . . . [   ]

9. The library
has a good librarian and is open after school hours . . . .+10

is crammed into an old storage area . . . .–5

has been taken over by the driver ed program . . . .–10

10. The school
is open to the community after regular classes . . . .+5

offers classes for adults and families . . . .+5

teaches its community's history and culture . . . .+5

practices a variety of teaching styles and techniques . . . .+5

has lots of field trips and out-of-school activities . . . .+5

offers assistance to students affected by drugs/alcohol, pregnancy, parenthood,
truancy, abuse, gangs, etc. . . . .+5

11. The school

offers an antidrug program but not drama classes ....–5

offers driving lessons but not civic lessons ....–5

offers JROTC but no mediation or peer conflict resolution ....–5

12. Students learn

how to ask searching questions ....+5

how to get around locker searches ....–5

how to write in a personal journal ....+5

how to write on the walls ....–5

how to argue persuasively with their parents ....+5

how to argue persuasively with their parole officers ....–5

13. For security and discipline the school uses

faculty, administrators, and the students ....+10

faculty and administrators ....+5

security guards ....–5

city police ....–10

13. Upon encountering a young person in the hall, a school official typically says something like

"Good morning, Jannine" ....+5

"I need to see your ID" ....–5

14. The school believes that students largely learn by

doing projects and discussing ....+10

sitting in rows and listening ....–10

15. In preparing for life after graduation, the school

is as interested in students not going to college as in those who are ....+5

concentrates on the needs of college-bound students ....–5

16. Deduct 3 points for every audiovisual aid or computer in the school that is *not* working ....[   ]

17. Extracurricular programs, such as the arts, sports, and skill-oriented clubs, are considered

an important part of what makes the school great ....+5

nice but in today's competitive environment as something that must give way to other things ....–5

18. BONUS: The school is

an inviting place that I would enjoy attending ....+20

GROW THINGS

Marcia Love of the Worldwatch Institute has noted that while the New York metropolitan region's population grew only 5 percent in 25 years, developed areas have increased by 61 percent, "consuming nearly a quarter of the region's open space, forests and farmlands."

Contradictory as it sounds, nature and wilderness are an essential part of a city. Not only do they contribute ecological balance, they offer solid social and economic advantages as well. Consider, for example, what would happen to the value of property surrounding New York's Central Park were that vast preserve suddenly to slip into a black hole. Consider the cost of providing alternative recreation space. The psychological effects on residents. The impact on tourism. And so forth.

Agriculture is important too. Much as the separation of work and community has created numerous urban costs and tensions, so the separation of food growing and its consumption has been expensive and counterproductive. Today the average food item in this country travels 1,300 miles from farm to supermarket. While it's true that the lettuce in the supermarket may be cheaper than that available at a local farmer's market, the former item's price does not include social costs, such as those involved in a system of migrant farm labor, the health consequences of pesticide use, the pollution from a truck driving 1,300 miles, and the taxpayer subsidy to the federal highway system. Increasingly, in fact, locally grown produce is beginning to be prominently displayed at supermarkets, a reflection of our changing values.

Urban growth boundaries: A major problem for cities is to preserve what they have not already destroyed. Oregon passed a law in 1973 that required each of the state's 242 cities to come up with a plan that used urban land efficiently while protecting surrounding farm and forest land. An urban growth boundary was established, and new development is prohibited or limited beyond this line. San Jose, California, did something similar in 1970. As a result the city nearly doubled in population without growing in territory. Both San Jose and Phoenix were cities of about 100,000 population in 1950, and both were spread over 17 square miles. Today San Jose has almost the population of Phoenix but takes up only 30 percent as much land.

Urban farming: Of course you can grow things inside the city as well. Hong King, one of the world's densest cities, grows 45 percent of its own vegetables. A survey of Harlem found 1,000 lots that might be used for urban gardens were they not filled with trash, toxic materials, and drug dealers. Harlem's agriculturists have had so much luck with existing projects that there's been some talk of establishing vineyards to produce Chardonnay de Harlem.

Farmers' markets: Cities could plan where their food will come from as carefully as where their residents will work. Farmers' markets, with their lower transportation costs, reduced packaging, and fresher food, need to be regarded as essential rather than merely quaint. While American farmers' markets have doubled in the past decade to 2,000, this is far short of the 62,000 such centers in Europe.

Getting rid of stuff: Of course the rest of the food chain needs attention as well. Rather than ship our waste someplace else, John Todd has proposed greenhouse-based sewage-purifying photosynthetic ecosystems, which "look and smell like a botanical garden." Todd's system for Harwich, Massachusetts, produced high-quality water with fecal coliform levels as low as one hundredth those allowable for swimming water.

Greening roofs: The city also needs to become much greener. Landscape architect Theodore Osmundson notes that in Stuttgart experts found that if roof gardens were increased by 15 percent to 20 percent, there would be a decrease in needed storm sewage capacity of 15 percent simply because of the gardens' temporary water retention after downpours. Berlin and some other German cities are now requiring the greening of the roofs of many new buildings.

MAKE IT EASIER FOR PEOPLE TO GET AROUND (AND STAY PUT).

The most efficient mass transit system: I once asked a transportation consultant to name the single most efficient mode of mass transit. His reply: "Stop people from moving around so much."

Nothing we could do with mass transit can match the effect of lessening the need for people to travel. One study, for example, has found that doubling the population density of a city reduces annual auto mileage per capita by 25 to 30 percent.

We resist such truths because of habit and because the nature of our cities teaches us to. As urban planner Edmund P. Fowler points out, "Our deconcentrated, segregated city has encouraged us to want mobility—the ability to get *to* what we need—rather than access, which is having what we need where we need it."

Fowler notes that in most large North American cities, "transportation and land use planning are carried out in completely different offices by completely different people." Further, "vast areas of the city remain largely unused during weekdays, and only come to life at night, or on weekends—or vice versa." We have often so distanced some of the institutions once considered essential to community, such as schools and recreation, that we actually end up commuting to them as well as to our work.

The second most efficient mass transit system: The bicycle is an amazingly efficient way to move people around. Through any given amount of space, you can move about twice as many people per hour by bike as you can by car, and 50 percent more than by bus, and they'll be healthier for it. In Japan 15 percent of all workers use bikes to commute. In Dutch cities the figure for *all* trips varies from 20 to 50 percent.

While getting people to make 20-mile commutes by bike would take some doing (especially during a midwestern winter), in fact almost 40 percent of all vehicle trips are under 2 miles. That's a 10- to 15-minute bike ride. Draw a map representing a 15-minute bike trip from where you are, and it will cover an area 36 times larger than that within a 15-minute walk.

Bikes not only are cheap, they can be free. Activists in Portland, Oregon, have been spray painting old bikes bright yellow and putting them out where anyone can use them.

The most inefficient mass transit system: It's the freeway. No one has come up with a sillier idea than carrying lone individuals in eight-foot-long, $25,000 vehicles down roadways that have become jammed and obsolete because of what planners call the iron law of traffic: *Traffic will increase to fill the space available to it.* One reason this law works so well is that people judge commuting by time and not by distance. Build a freeway, and people will just drive to town from farther away.

Light rail: The streetcar's demise came in no small part because it competed too effectively with the automobile. It is now being revived in a form called light rail. Light rail has many advantages: It disperses development, costs far less to build than subways, doesn't create land speculation in its wake, and physically takes space from the automobile.

The bus: Exclusive bus lanes can be easily and cheaply created on major arteries, especially if they run counter to the flow of automobile traffic. Buses can be made more efficient by being given priority (through use of school bus–type flashing stoplights) when pulling in and out of bus stops. Buses can have exterior bike racks to encourage mixed-mode use, as is done in Portland, Seattle, and a number of California cities. Buses can be equipped with zappers to control signal lights. Through such efforts, urban bus transportation might become as least as good as the shuttle bus service at the average airport or theme park.

Taxis and jitneys: The taxi can be a major form of mass transit, and subsidized taxi service can be used

> We want a well-lit neighborhood. All alleys shall be painted white or yellow. . . . All trees will be properly trimmed and maintained. . . . New trees will be planted to increase the beauty of our neighborhoods. . . . [All schools will] completely upgrade the bathrooms, making them more modern, provide a bathroom monitor to each bathroom which will provide freshen-up toiletries at a minimum cost to the students.
> —From a post-riot plan for L.A. drawn up by the Bloods and Crips gangs

as a substitute for buses on routes where ridership wouldn't justify the larger vehicles. A jitney is a cross between a bus and a taxi, an overgrown hack that moves along a predetermined route. Jitneys were common in this country until the streetcar companies got them outlawed. In places like NYC and Miami they have made a comeback—illegally—and are one of the most underused and worthwhile modes of urban transport.

Walking: Many cities are not pedestrian-friendly. Inviting pathways, propedestrian traffic laws, and density of construction could all increase the amount of walking people do.

The automobile: Even the automobile could play a more respectable role in an ecologically oriented transportation system. Architect Patrick Hare, for example, has found that Washington, D.C.'s Shirley Highway's high-occupancy vehicle lanes carry more than three times as many people as the road's four other lanes. The HOV lane users save an average of 20 minutes' travel time each way. Hare would like to establish HOV lanes on urban streets where there's a need to cut back traffic.

CLEAN THE PLACE UP.

It is hard to create better communities if they continue to carry the hallmarks of their neglected past. Planting grass, bushes, and trees is an easy and quick way to declare a community's intent to rebuild itself. Cities could provide these, as well as free paint for external spruce-ups. Graffiti could be discouraged by encouraging murals.

Yes, this is cosmetic. You do it for the same reason you wash your face or put on lipstick in the morning: to make yourself feel better about all the other things you have to do. If the devil is in the details of urban life, then so is the salvation. And a wise city would have plenty of paint and grass seed to give that first outward and visible sign of an inward determination to change things.

HAVE SOMETHING FOR EVERYONE.

Much of what has been described here involves little more than the rediscovery of urban practices and habits that existed during the great growth era of the American city. We have in recent decades been so intent on making our cities neat and orderly that we have forgotten that the major contribution of the city is its explosive and random potential. Our goal has been physical order and fiscal benefits; the results have been social disorder and huge deficits.

A thriving urban ecology should be not just about clean air and trees but also about communities and economic survival, justice, decent education, security, happiness, the joy of chance, variety, and opportunity.

In the end cities are not just places but, as Brown University's Arnold Weinstein puts it, "work being done." Free from the predetermined human and physical geography of a rural or small-town community, we find in them a chance to design our own environment, create our own lives, and do our own business. Cities often fail us, but it is their enduring service to both shelter and venture that makes even the grimmest among them continuing magnets.

So even as those who have used them well leave for some place grander, quieter, or safer, the retiree and the suburban-bound professional are replaced by a young artist, a drug dealer cashing in his chips for a legal business, an ambitious new immigrant, a recent college grad, or an entrepreneur. And the urban story begins again.

An American Parts List

800 news conferences annually at the
National Press Club

37,000 movie theaters

110,000 schools

162,000 garages and auto repair shops

82 million bicyclists

13 million citizens who have been homeless at some
point in their lives

9. How to stay safe & play fair
Without locking everyone else up

How did *you* stay out of jail anyway?

How did you manage to stay out of jail anyway? Or, as most of you up-standing, wonderful readers are probably more accustomed to being asked, how did you become so successful? Or become such a fine citizen? Or do so well in school?

In any case, we can pretty well guess what some of the answers might be: good parents, a happy home, a terrific school, adults who showed you how to do things and who supported you and offered wisdom when you needed it, a community that expected certain things of you and gave you much in return, perhaps even a special place like a library or playground or summer camp that helped you become who you are. We can also pretty well guess that absent from your list will be the name of a parole officer, prison, cop, or judge.

> We imprison five times as many people per capita as Canada and seven times as many as most European countries, yet we have similar crime rates.

If you are a parent, think also of the things you do to guide your children into productive, happy, and decent adulthood. Think of what's available—schools, sports leagues and extracurricular activities—to help to make that possible. How often have you called on the cops to assist?

Now let us go across town, to the neighborhoods of kids whom sociologists and the media describe as "at risk" or part of a "permanent underclass." By such language, and before we even get there, we have given a verdict and assumed defeat. The unspoken question becomes: How did you stay out of jail anyway?

Values without support

In fact, once you start looking closely at these neighborhoods, you discover that the biggest difference is not in their values but in their ability to express them and pass them on.

The people living in these communities are mostly normal people in abnormal circumstances. To be sure, such communities have an excess of social deviants, but they are deviants of their own community's norms as well as those of America in general.

Go to one of America's poorer neighborhoods, and you're likely to find more decency and morality than in your average congressional hearing room or corporate board meeting. But there are some other things that you might find as well:

- No uniforms for high school sports teams
- Sporadic gunfire and drive-by shootings
- A nearby crack house that the city won't close because it is owned by a major mayoral campaign contributor
- Poor housing abysmally maintained by public and private landlords
- Buckets in classrooms to catch the water from leaky school roofs

---

WHEN'S A MINORITY NOT A MINORITY?

In prison. Blacks constitute about 12 percent of the U.S. population and about 13 percent of all drug users. BUT:

- More than half the people now in prison are black.
- Black Americans constitute 35 percent of drug arrestees, 55 percent of those convicted on drug possession charges, and 74 percent of all those sentenced to prison in drug cases.
- Since the early 1980s arrests of whites on drug charges have increased 49 percent; arrests of blacks have gone up 156 percent
- A study of California's "three strikes" law found that blacks were being arrested at a rate 13 times that of whites.

- No after-school programs
- Inadequate childcare programs
- A recreation center, no longer staffed because of budget cuts, taken over by drug dealers

In short, many of the normal tools, places, and programs for building a successful and happy life are simply missing or in terrible shape. Those who make it in such communities must do so without the assets many of the rest of us take for granted.

Finding substitutes for things that work

In these less blessed communities we typically provide a substitute for all these tools, places, and programs. We call it law enforcement. It seldom works well, frequently kills someone, and usually ends up costing us a lot of money. This is not because the police are ineffective or because we are not "tough on crime." We are simply asking the police to do far too much. Throughout history community order has largely grown out of the cooperation and effectiveness of individuals, schools, and families and the strength of local institutions. The police have been there not to maintain order, or even to define it, but to assist and protect the community and to intervene in those rare cases the normal community systems can't handle. One should not expect the fire department to come over and cook your dinner safely or light the logs in your fireplace, nor should one expect the police to replace the normal functions of individuals, families, and community institutions. Yet that is precisely what we have done.

> You do not willy-nilly arrest a father in front of a son, or break into someone's house looking for some kind of minor drug deal and throw everyone onto the floor in front of screaming children and upset mothers and drag people off the way we now do routinely in our inner cities without having it come back at you. You create anger. You nurture alienation.
> —Criminologist Jerome Miller in *Utne Reader*

Many police officers understand this better than politicians and the press. As one put it, "What the police do is make arrests, and we already have more arrests than we know what to do with." In my hometown of Washington,

- When San Francisco banned smoking in its jail, the price of a pack of cigarettes went up to $120. The same thing has happened with drugs thanks to drug prohibition.
- Around the turn of the century, heroin and aspirin were legal and cost about the same. Today aspirin costs 20 cents a gram at a drugstore; heroin costs $70 a gram and up out on the streets.
- When a Liverpool doctor started giving heroin to addicts in 1982, the number of new addicts in the city dropped. Meanwhile, there was a 12-fold increase in neighboring towns. The difference: Liverpool addicts no longer needed to encourage new drug use in order to have enough customers to pay for their own habits.

D.C., we arrest and lock up more people up on a per capita basis than any other city in the country, yet we remain high in the crime tallies. I once walked with a cop through a decrepit public housing project. "They never ask the police before they build places like this," he said. But even a tough cop can't make a politician tender at election time or an editorial writer rational on a slow news day. The truth is that pretending you're fighting crime pays. It pays for politicians trying to win an election. It pays for media seeking to shock and titillate. It pays for police bureaucrats trying to maintain their budgets, and it pays for a burgeoning prison industry. Too often, however, it does not pay where it counts: in cutting crime.

The high cost of being scared

There is far less mystery to crime and crime fighting than we are led to believe. In fact, there's even less crime than we've been led to believe. Between 1985 and 1995, for example, property crime dropped about 5 percent. The murder rate has stayed remarkably steady for the past 20 years. Yet since 1980 the number of people we have put in prison has tripled.

But such facts are consistently ignored by the politicians and the media because there is more advantage—for audience and for votes—in keeping the public riled up and scared. So riled up, for example, that during the 1980s the state of California built 16 new prisons but only 1 new state university campus. So riled up that we are willing to pay for the equivalent of 3 new 500-bed prisons opening every week.

How not to wage a war on drugs

By the 1980s drug use in America had peaked. Marijuana use was one half what it had been in the late seventies. During the Carter years, in fact, drug treatment efforts were so successful that heroin overdose deaths dropped by two thirds.

> Our strategy of punishing drug addicts is akin to expelling from school students with learning disabilities.
> —Eric Sterling, Criminal Justice Foundation

But by 1985, with public drug facilities losing funds under the Reagan budgetary cutbacks, the figures started climbing back up. Those who could not afford private treatment were being hurt most, and drug overdose deaths in major cities climbed 18 percent over the previous decade.

It was enough of an excuse for President Reagan to declare yet another war on drugs. There was no subtlety in this. The *Washington Times* reported, "President Reagan yesterday declared drug dealers a greater national security threat than terrorists," and *U.S. News & World Report* flatly declared that narcotics had turned "into a national security threat.

Ralph Salerno was a New York City cop who became a specialist on the mob and a consultant to other police departments. A few years ago Salerno was training a grand jury that was looking into organized crime in the Fort Lauderdale area. He told the group that police estimate they seize, at most, 10 percent of the drugs being sold.

As Salerno described it to Pacific News Service, "I said to them, 'Suppose Ralph Salerno could wave a magic wand and stop 20 percent of the drugs coming into Broward County from coming in. How many of you would be in favor of that?' All 22 or 23 of them raised their hands.

"I then asked, 'What happens to the price of the 80 percent that is getting through?' And one gentleman—a businessman—said it would probably go up. And I said, 'You're probably right. So what would happen to the statistics of breaks and entries and tape decks ripped out of cars and CB radios stolen and little old ladies knocked down on the ground while someone grabs their pocket book and runs away?' And they said, 'My God, they would go up.'

"One and a half minutes into that educational exercise I asked the same people, how many of you would now like to see me wave my magic wand and cut off 20 percent of the drugs. And they all voted against it."

Headlines, police blotters, death certificates testify to a nation on a binge."

Ironically, the renewed growth in urban drug use was being fueled by steps already undertaken by the Reaganites. The administration had early gone after marijuana, the hardest drug to hide. That it was also the most benign, causing less harm than either tobacco or alcohol, was ignored. As pressure was placed on the marijuana trade, prices rose and availability declined. An economic vacuum for a cheap street drug was created and then quickly filled by international and domestic drug traffickers. Thus the first accomplishment of the Reagan war on drugs became access to a new and less expensive form of cocaine, crack.

It was not an auspicious beginning. The war was quickly accompanied by a murder rate that rose with drug arrests. The number of murders in D.C., for example, more than doubled in three years. It is hard, in fact, to think of another domestic policy that has caused so much mayhem in such a short period as the war on drugs.

Even today, though, only a tiny handful of politicians will publicly admit what Minneapolis Police Chief Anthony Bouza said back in 1988: "All of the action, in Minneapolis or elsewhere, is just spinning a wheel and chasing our own tails. It ain't working." Or what former Kansas City and San Jose Police Chief Joseph McNamara said in 1996: "The police should not be wasting scarce resources arresting a half million or so people every year for marijuana offenses."

Mayor Kurt Schmoke of Baltimore is an exception. He points out that the drug problem is really three problems: drug addiction, violence, and AIDs transmittal by users. He likes to ask people three questions:

THE SNITCH EXPLOSION

Increasingly citizens are being dragged into criminal matters in which they have little or no role. A few examples:

- In Utah business owners were threatened with contempt actions if they refused to tell the police who had been driving speeding company trucks caught by photo radar. Individual citizens were forced to reveal drivers' names under threat of jail. Said one lawyer: "It's a way of intimidating people into informing on their families and friends."
- The Supreme Court has ruled that the government can seize cars or houses used in a crime, even if the owner of the property had nothing to do with the crime.

- Have we won the war on drugs?
- Do you think we *are* winning the war on drugs?
- Do you think that doing more of what we are doing will win the war on drugs?

In the late 1960s there were 2 federal agencies enforcing the drug laws on a budget less than $10 million. Today there are 50 agencies splitting a $15 billion budget.

In each case, says Schmoke, most people answer no. Why not, he then says, take a look at some other solutions?

Unintended consequences

While the war on drugs hasn't stopped the flow of drugs, it has had other effects, such as encouraging drive-by shootings, assaults in schools, and ran-

FIRST STEPS TO A SANE DRUG POLICY

1. Treat drug addiction as a public health issue rather than a criminal matter.
2. Put the surgeon general in charge.
3. Make clean needle exchanges for addicts legal and routine.
4. Greatly increase funds for treatment.
5. Get the military out of civilian drug law enforcement.
6. Stop arresting persons for being addicted and possessing the drugs to feed their addiction. Get them help.
7. Allow doctors to run heroin maintenance programs.
8. End most drug testing, replacing it where necessary for safety reasons with skill impairment tests, which are far more inclusive and useful.
9. End all unconstitutional practices related to the drug wars such as jump-out squads and coerced warrantless searches.
10. End the vast ethnic disparities in the enforcement of drug laws.

dom attacks on innocent persons. It has also increased the military's intrusion into civilian life and encouraged a wholesale dismantling of 4th Amendment protections against unreasonable search and seizure.

Because white middle-class citizens do not match the police profile of a drug courier, nor are likely to be found near a center city drug market, nor live close enough to crack houses to have their doors mistakenly broken down by a SWAT team, there remains the stunningly inaccurate myth that somehow we have not been tough enough on urban crime. The reality is that the fastest-growing public housing program in America is prison construction.

Cops as a management tool

A few years ago Washington, D.C., became concerned over the increase in guns and violence in its schools. With great fanfare, the mayor announced a program that would add more police officers to those schools that had experienced the most significant upsurge, expand locker searches, and so forth. There was general acceptance of the notion that escalating the police presence was the right approach.

Few noticed that there were other schools, also in high crime areas, that had not experienced unusual violence, nor were they under intense police patrol. Why were these schools different? I asked the chief of security for the schools. Without hesitation he replied, "Good management." In other words, the city was using the police to compensate not just for violent kids, but for poor principals as well.

Learning how to deal with adjacent human beings

Despite our growing use of the police to replace the former functions of neighborhood institutions, the drive for family and community still remains so strong that some of the young have created a surrogate for what has disappeared. They call it a gang.

As one social worker, Mike Francis, explains it, gangs "have clearly satisfied some needs that family and community have not met for these kids." One might assume that if subteens and teens can with such

ease find a substitute for missing communal aspects of life, adults might be able to offer an even more attractive alternative. Unfortunately, in too many cases, the adult response is to ignore the cry for community, respect, and meaning and to respond to the young simply with more force.

On the other hand, the imaginative introduction of positive alternatives can have encouraging results. One of the most significant of these is the teaching of mediation and conflict resolution. A teacher in this field, Kathy Owen, notes that many of the young simply lack the skills or language to respond other than physically to being "dissed." Her own work has been so successful that one of her high school students, upon hearing a bus driver and passenger in the midst of a heated dispute, walked to the front of the bus and announced, "I am a trained mediator. I think I can help you." And she did.

Sports can also help. In fact, it is hard to think of many better ways to break the cultural grip of violence among young urban males than with a major improvement in school sports and after-school recreation programs. Certainly it is preferable to cutting recreation department funding and watching rec centers being taken over by drug dealers. Coaches and roving recreation department leaders can also be desperately needed intermediaries between the young and the often hated police. During the sixties roving leaders acted as combination coaches and community organizers. The former skill complemented the latter since coaches are after all the ultimate organizers. Like a number of worthy spin-offs of the War on Poverty, however, the use of roving leaders has unfortunately declined.

Of course, the real answer is an economic alternative to robbery and drugs. An activist who has helped end strife among members of five gangs—no mean feat—reports that the young men see the McDonaldization of the economy as a dead end; what they want, and would be willing to change habits for, is training that would lead to skilled jobs. At present, neither the training nor the jobs are there.

> In March we began, as usual, the spring ritual of teaching, not baseball, but basic strategies for dealing with adjacent human beings; i.e., it is not always necessary to respond to one's own failure by knocking the hell out of the guy next to you if he's smaller than you, or by hurling a bottle or a rock at him if he's bigger; i.e., there are other ways to deal with a friend's failure than to jeer gleefully at his inadequacy; i.e., it's not necessary to point out, every half hour, that a classmate's mother is a drunk or that his father is in jail or that his sister is pregnant. . . . Baseball is the ideal forum for teaching the art of failure because failure is endemic to the sport; the very best at any level fail to get a hit seven out of ten times.
> —Little League Coach Sam Dunn in annual letter to team supporters

Putting the community back in charge

What law enforcement tool do every shopping mall and big office building have—but not most neighborhoods?

Their own police force.

It is hard to imagine how we can restore order to our communities without giving them some role in creating and maintaining this order.

Think, for example, about what typically happens when a kid first

From 9:30 A.M. to 2 P.M. every weekday social worker Dawnel White gets the tough cases: women for whom some other form of treatment (and even law enforcement) has failed: prostitutes, drug addicts, abusive or neglectful mothers targeted by child protective services. White's approach is to help these women, for the first time in their lives, create a community.

It is not a passive community. It is neither punitive nor permissive. It offers, as one woman put it, a "sense of safety," but it's also work. White tells the women they are in her program to "clear the wreckage of the past." The women each pay at least one dollar a week to belong. They are expected to follow program rules (from "No drinking or drugging" to "One person will talk at a time") and to deal with those who break them. Sometimes a rule breaker will suggest her own penalty, but typically the group decides after a lengthy discussion. Among the consequences: setting up chairs for meetings, taking out trash, or writing papers on topics such as "How my actions speak louder than words."

The women learn to listen to one another, earn and give respect, control anger, talk about spiritual matters, and become part of a community, starting with the one they are slowly building for themselves.

gets into trouble—minor shoplifting, vandalism, a fight. The police are called to the scene. And what do the police do? They remove the young person from the very community against which the crime has been committed. The implicit message is that your sin is against the city or the county or the state, not against your neighbors or your community. Thus from the very start we teach the wrong lesson. The lessons can sometimes be cruelly absurd. In Pennsylvania, following passage of a law providing for expulsion of students carrying not only guns and knives but any "cutting instrument," some youths found themselves arrested for possession of such items as scissors and nail clippers.

Imagine instead that the community had its own constables—with police training and powers—who lived in the community, were known in the community, and helped the community maintain its own order. In minor nonviolent offenses the first person on the scene would be the constable, who could quickly bring the offender before a community justice board instead of waiting months for the matter to wend its way through the normal-downtown judicial labyrinth. If found guilty, the offender would have to provide restitution or perform community service.

This is not daydreaming. The spring 1994 issue of *Policy Review* described the system of *elected* constables in Houston, Texas. One of these constables was Victor Trevino, who managed—with the help of over 200 volunteer deputies—to cut the crime rate 10 percent, arrest nearly 2,000 wanted parole violators, slash the school truancy rate in half and bring back Little League after a 25-year absence. Trevino, the first Latino immigrant elected in Harris County, worked in an inner-city community of 150,000 people. All his volunteers were fully trained and had the arrest powers of regular officers.

Nor is the notion of community-based restorative justice untested. Writing in the *Progressive Review,* David Spero described how western New York's Genesee County found itself with overflowing jail cells. It turned to community service sentences and to recruiting nonprofits, schools, churches, and road crews to assign hard work in lieu of jail time. As Spero notes, for the criminals working with such institutions it "was often their first positive contact with anyone in authority."

Then the county developed a system of victim support, including restitution from offenders. A felon diversion program allowed screened offenders a chance to put their lives together while their cases were put on hold. Only 5 percent of those in the program turned out to be repeat offenders. Spero describes one case: "An 18-year-old sniper on LSD seriously wounded two passersby. He went through diversion for 18 months, including victim-offender conciliation. This conciliation helps victims heal and forces offenders to confront the pain they have caused. The young sniper finally received a short jail sentence plus community service and now works, pays taxes, and raises a family in Genesee County."

Communities can get involved in other ways, as in the victim-offender mediation program of L.A.'s Centinela Valley. Director Steve Goldsmith told Spero how it works: "First we get the victim to agree to mediation, then the young offenders and their parents. We hold the sessions at a place convenient to the victim, with two volunteer mediators who have gone through 40 hours of free training. The mediators let the victim and offender work out the solution. The important thing is the kids have to hear the consequences of their actions on others."

Such programs take a lot of effort. There are about 200 volunteer sponsors and victim advocates in the Genesee program and more than a 100 community agencies working with offenders.

Yet there is no substitute for organic social order. We can't just call the cops and think everything will be taken care of.

Who really gets away with it

David Burnham, author of *Above the Law,* a tough look at the U.S. Justice Department, has conducted the most comprehensive examination of how America's top prosecutors really function. Using computerized records as well more conventional journalistic sources, Burnham came up with some disturbing data:

- Of all people indicted on federal charges in 1994, 38 percent were charged with drug violations. One half of 1 percent was charged with crimes involving the environment, occupational safety, health, and product or consumer safety matters. This doesn't mean people don't commit such crimes. In fact, the *National Law Journal* did a survey of lawyers for major corporations and found that two thirds of them believed their companies had violated federal or state environmental laws in the past year.

> **WHAT GETS PROSECUTED**
>
> Journalist David Burnham found that in 1994 the U.S. government prosecuted the following percentages of cases that came to its attention:
>
> - Immigration cases: 83 percent
> - Drug cases: 53 percent
> - White-collar crime: 30 percent
> - Civil rights cases: less than 5 percent

- There is little consistency in the application of the law. For example, between 1981 and 1990 there were no criminal pollution cases filed in the Northern District of California. In San Diego there were many. The lawyer who had been U.S. attorney for the Northern District at the time claimed by way of explanation, "There is no pollution in the Northern District." Similarly, if you want to do drugs, you'll be safest in Las Vegas, San Francisco, Los Angeles, or Nashville. The feds in these areas aren't that interested compared with other locales. Explains Burnham, antidrug activity there "upsets the tourists."

☞ Since 1970 some 200,000 workers have died in the workplace, but only one business executive has gone to prison for violations of federal occupational safety and health laws.

Call a good architect and you may not need 911

Physical factors are important in urban safety. Front porches keep watch on the street. Planner Edmund Fowler found in his studies that juvenile crime rises in blocks that are too long or lack diversity of use. And Canadians Gerda R. Wekerle and Carolyn Whitzman, in a book entitled *Safe Cities,* argue that relying heavily on law and order "kills the city it is purporting to save. It deepens the divisions and the fear of the 'other' which are among the most harmful effects of fear of crime." Among their alternatives: detailed safety audits of communities, parks, and buildings. Here are just a few of the questions the pair would have neighborhoods raise as they conduct these audits:

☑ If the place is to be used at night, can you identify a face at fifteen yards?
☑ Does street lighting shine on pedestrian pathways and possible danger spots rather than on the street?
☑ Are light fixtures protected from casual vandalism?
☑ Are blind corners avoided?
☑ Are entrances to housing hidden or set in?
☑ Are there good sight lines in stairwells and lobby entrances?
☑ Can laundry rooms or storage areas be moved to places of higher activity?
☑ Are there signs telling where to get help?
☑ Are stores that stay open late clustered together?

Wekerle and Whitzman believe America is well behind Europe and the British Commonwealth in making its cities physically safe. The United States relies on law and order after the fact rather than on good planning ahead of time. The two approaches are not mutually exclusive, and neither is a substitute for dealing with root causes, but the balance in America is badly askew.

Just the facts

In 1994 the National Criminal Justice Commission, a private nonpartisan group, released the first detailed independent study of our justice system since the Kerner Commission in the 1960s. Here are a few of its findings:

- Every year more people are arrested and jailed for a few days than the entire combined population of our 13 smallest states.
- The growth of the justice system has had little, if any, effect on crime.
- A state's rate of incarceration has little or no correlation with its crime rate.
- The nation spends about $100 billion annually on law enforcement—more than the entire combined federal budgets for Head Start, job training programs, AFDC, housing assistance, and food stamps.
- The average cost of incarcerating a 20-year-old for life is $1.8 million.
- Prison costs are rising faster than any other category of state spending.
- Most offenders are not dangerous. Only 3 percent of reported offenses result in any physical injury.
- Of state prison inmates, 53 percent are doing time for crimes that Americans deem "petty," such as shoplifting $10 worth of merchandise or smoking marijuana.
- Many defense contractors are converting to civilian law enforcement.
- An expanding law enforcement industry—including new prisons and products—increases expenditures regardless of need or effectiveness.
- Relative to their population, there are seven times as many minorities in prison as whites.
- In many cities about half of young African American men are under the control of the criminal justice system in some way.
- Women represent the fastest-growing classification of prisoners nationwide, with most offenses being nonviolent property crimes, such as shoplifting, check forgery, or substance abuse.

Anatomy of a crime wave

Between 1985 and 1988, in the wake of the revived drug war, murders in Washington, D.C. soared from 145 a year to 369. During this period the city's Office of Criminal Justice Planning did an unusually detailed analysis of homicides. The report illustrates dramatically the complexity of crime and shows why simple or overarching solutions rarely work. For example, here's a chart that indicates who was most and least likely to be killed during this period:

FIGURING THE ODDS
Percent of Murders in Each Category
1985–88 in Washington, D.C.

Least likely	Most likely
Victim under 18 (8%)	Victim 18–25(30%)
Victim a white female (1%)*	Victim a black male (75%)
Murders in richest ward (1%)†	Murders in poorest ward (20%)
No drugs or alcohol in body (37%)	Drugs or alcohol in body (63%)
July (5 percent)	January or June (12%)
Thursday (11%)	Saturday (17%)
6–9 A.M. (7%)	9 P.M.–midnight (25%)

In short, it was virtually impossible to be killed in Washington if you were a young white girl living in upscale Georgetown on an early Thursday morning in July. If, on the other hand, you were a young black 20-year-old male living in low-income Anacostia and dealing drugs on a Saturday night in June, your chances of being killed were far greater than the overall statistics would suggest. And if you were not buying or selling drugs at all, your chances of being killed in D.C. were about the same as in Copenhagen.

Other differences showed up, most strikingly in motive. The murder rate resulting from altercations or robberies actually dropped substantially during this period and those that stemmed from domestic violence stayed about the same. But those involving drugs leaped over 300 percent! Clearly one result of stepping up the war on drugs had been a huge increase in murder.

Meanwhile, other crimes took their own course. Rape dropped 55 percent, robbery dropped slowly and then started climbing, and so forth. The

*White females constitute about 15 percent of the city's population; black males about 30 percent
†Each ward contained about 13 percent of the population.

nature of, and motives for, crime rarely stay fixed, however. For example, the violence that grew out of the war on drugs, while failing to eliminate the drug culture, did encourage a new culture of violence. Now drugs are not needed for there to be motivation for killing someone; a simple insult will do.

Road Signs

23 violent acts per hour on Saturday morning children's television

248,000 lawsuits filed in federal court annually

740,000 lawyers

80,000 armed private security guards in L.A. County

16,567 sheriff's deputies and LAPD officers in L.A. County

220 million guns

2 million violent crimes a year

1.2 million prisoners

276,000 shoplifters caught in 1995

928 shots fired at suspects by NYC cops in 1993, 173 of which hit their target

160,000 state and federal jury trials every year

15 children killed by firearms every day

A crime buster's checklist

☑ Is your city's homicide squad adequately staffed, trained, and funded? Does your police department concentrate on violent crime?

☑ How well trained is your police force? How do its arrests stack up in court? How often are cases thrown out on legal grounds?

☑ Do your police officers have easy access to legal advice? Most American police officers are expected to enforce the law with only a slim understanding of it.

☑ Are your police and courts adequately insulated from local politics?

☑ Is the law enforced fairly and equitably in all parts of town? Do the police consider some citizens more equal than others?

☑ Are officers polite and respectful in their dealings with citizens, no matter what their ethnicity or income level? This is not just a matter of civil liberties or a nicety; it greatly increases the willingness of citizens to provide assistance to the police.

☑ Has your city or town done a careful analysis of crime that details the demographics, geography, and other factors determining when, where, and how crimes are committed? Is this information available to the public?

☑ Has your community done a safety audit of parks, passageways, stairs, and other spaces? Have you done a safety audit of your home? Place of work?

☑ Are sex criminals in your state or community given treatment while in prison? Is treatment available to sex offenders on probation or parole? A year's worth of intensive treatment can be provided for a quarter to two thirds of the cost of holding someone in prison for a year.

☑ Does your community have an effective civilian review board to deal with citizen complaints against police officers?

☑ What percent of cases does your police department solve? Nationwide, for example, unsolved homicides rose from 14 percent of all cases in 1970 to 33 percent in the 1993. Only a quarter of all robberies are solved, and only 13 percent of all burglaries.

☑ Are there active citizen patrols in high crime neighborhoods?

☑ Do prisoners have easy access to condoms? America's prisons have become ideal incubators for AIDS.

☑ Are the names of warrant jumpers publicized? Is there a squad specifically assigned to enforce warrants?

☑ Does your neighborhood have crime-encouraging physical characteristics, such as long blocks, uniform buildings, and lack of diversity in their use?

A CRIME BUSTER'S POLICE CHIEF

Nicholas Pastore is the highly regarded police chief of New Haven, Connecticut. Here a few of his thoughts about policing:

- Meanspirited policing leads to mean streets.
- To expect others to play by the rules, the police must do so as well.
- Police leaders must admit that traditional hard-line approaches have failed.
- Public leaders who pander to the call to get tough on crime limit police effectiveness and create conflicts between the police and the communities they serve.
- Police don't only enforce the law and jail people. They provide human services. Police "make house calls to every address, day or night. They go where others dare not go and serve people who have been ignored."
- If you keep filling up the jails, you will soon have a significant segment of society that is prison-influenced and prison-behaved.
- Arrest is a sign of failure by the police.
- Seventy percent of New Haven's police work would be unnecessary if drug prohibition were ended and there were enough treatment centers.

☑ To what other uses could drug hot spots be put? If one is an empty lot, could it be converted into community gardens? If it is an abandoned store or building, has the owner been approached to work out an alternative use? Could a sidewalk café be established to provide more activity on the street?

When it's the law that's wrong

William Penn may have thought he had settled the matter. Arrested in 1670 for preaching Quakerism, Penn was brought to trial. Despite Penn's admitting the charge, 4 of the 12 jurors voted to acquit. The judge sent the 4 to jail "without meat, drink, fire and tobacco" for failing to find Penn guilty. On appeal, however, the jurors' action was upheld, and the right of juries to judge both the law and the facts—to nullify the law if they chose—became part of British constitutional law.

It became part of American law as well, but you'd never know it listening to jury instructions today almost anywhere in the country. With only a few exceptions, juries are explicitly or implicitly told to worry only about the facts and let the

Alexander Hamilton's advice to cops

While I recommend in the strongest terms to the respective officers, activity, vigilance and firmness, I feel no less solicitude that their deportment may be marked with prudence, moderation and good temper.

They will bear in mind that their countrymen are freemen, and as such are impatient of everything that bears the least mark of domineering spirit. They will, therefore refrain, with the most guarded circumspection, from whatever has the semblance of hautiness, rudeness or insult. If obstacles occur, they will remember that they are under the particular protection of the laws and they can meet with nothing disagreeable in the execution of their duty which these will not severely reprehend.

This reflection, and regard to the good of the service, will prevent at all times a spirit of irritation or resentment. They will endeavor to overcome difficulties, if any are experienced, by a cool and temperate perseverance in their duty— by address and moderation rather than by vehemence and violence.
> —From Alexander Hamilton's instructions to the first officers of the Revenue Marine, forerunner of the U.S. Coast Guard

judge decide the law. The right of jury nullification has become one of the legal system's best-kept secrets.

The theory behind nullification is simple: that the jury may, in a particular case, veto the use of a law it considers cruel, unreasonable, undemocratic, or otherwise defective.

Merely raising the issue of nullification makes prosecutors nervous, for it takes only one person who is aware of that right to hang a jury. Despite the

> If a juror accepts as the law that which the judge states then that juror has accepted the exercise of absolute authority of a government employee and has surrendered a power and right that once was the citizen's safeguard of liberty—for the saddest epitaph which can be carved in the memory of a vanished liberty is that it was lost because its possessors failed to stretch forth a saving hand while yet there was time.
>
> —Thomas Jefferson

refusal of courts to inform juries of their prerogative, American juries have periodically exercised it anyway.

Challenging a judge can be risky. Judges might ask jurors a question such as "Will you take the law as I give it?," implying that not only can you not question the law, but you can't even question the judge's interpretation of it. I have twice been dismissed from jury pools in pot possession cases during voir dire after telling the judge that I did not believe in punishing someone for having the health problem of drug addiction. After the second instance I asked a couple of prosecutors (both ex-defense attorneys) if I really had to tell the judge my feelings. They said that if she had found out about my public stance on drugs and jury nullification during the trial, it might have resulted not only in my dismissal as a juror but in a mistrial. If she had found out after the trial, she might have held me in contempt of court.

In recent years some peace protesters have been acquitted despite strong evidence that they violated the law. In the 19th century northern juries sometimes refused to convict under the Fugitive Slave Laws. And in 1735 journalist Peter Zenger, accused of seditious libel, was acquitted by a jury that ignored the court's instructions on the law, a case that laid the foundation for America's free press.*

Those who have endorsed the right of a jury to judge both the law and the facts include Chief Justice John Jay, Samuel Chase, Dean Roscoe Pound, Learned Hand, and Oliver Wendell Holmes.

Nullification has played a little-noted but significant role in the advance of religious and press freedom, the abolition of slavery, and the building of a labor movement. Even in the face of hostility by contemporary courts, it

---

*The O. J. Simpson criminal trial verdict, much reportage notwithstanding, was not a case of jury nullification. In the Simpson trial the jury found the evidence and not the law lacking.

has cropped up in political protest trials of the past few decades. And it might have surfaced more frequently in the absence of that hostility. The nullification principle involves the power to say no to the excesses of government and thus serves as a final defense against tyranny.

Getting the law out of our lives

> I tell employers that all personal contact has to cease. Employers have to be careful not to say anything personal and to have a witness in the room when there is social conversation.
>
> —Attorney who specializes in sexual harassment cases
> describing how businesses can avoid them

This matter-of-fact advice is just one more example of how we are creating a society based on what has been called automated distrust. In recent years we have been taught increasingly to think of employees as potential drug addicts, teachers as possible child molesters, tenants as probable building wreckers, and bosses as protorapists. We have institutionalized our fears in laws and in mandatory drug testing and in fingerprinting and in lengthy leases and in not conversing unless there are others in the room and in new categories of insurance to protect ourselves from other Americans who have been been taught to fear the same things.

Much of this concern is scary, unpredictable, expensive, and unproductive—not to mention crazy and inhuman. To be safe, one is not allowed unwitnessed social conversation with one's employer? What's going on here? A self-imposed lockdown of the soul?

When you examine such excesses, you often find two things:

- ☞ A serious societal problem, such as sexual harassment on the job
- ☞ A complex, adversarial, punitive, and often ineffective solution that is advocated in a spirit of retribution rather than remediation and is crafted by lawyers acting as either legislators or lobbyists. Our solutions tend to be highly inconsistent as well. Thus we wink at sexual abuse involving, say, a president or a Supreme Court justice, but pillory for offensive language some dolt of a corporate manager still trying to live up to the macho ideals drilled into him by his high school football coach.

So powerful have lawyers become that many people often assume that their solutions are the only ones that available. In fact, in some instances the solution not only fails to solve the original problem but makes matters worse. The would-be reformers also unwittingly contribute to the creation of a society in which everyone suspects everyone else. The problem with such reformers, G. K. Chesterton once noted, is that they slay St. George and leave the dragon.

The consequences of our overreliance on legal remedies have become particularly noticeable (and controversial) in situations where the law is directed not only at criminal actions but at undesired cultural behavior as well. While the law finds it relatively easy to define the former, it has, in areas such as antisocial conduct related to sex and race, settled for mushy wording and amibiguous directions to enforce a cultural course change, in many instances saying, in effect, let the courts decide.

Not only does this approach ignore the principle that laws should first be understandable, but it presumes that the law is the best tool to produce the desired change. There is little evidence of this.

The law, for example, can prohibit sin, but it cannot enforce virtue. Behind sexual harassment, racial discrimination, and homophobia lies a lack of respect for other humans, often based on cultural lessons learned early in life. The law by its nature cannot say that if you do not respect others, this is what will happen to you, so it tries to define forms of disrespect and outlaw them one by one. Inevitably the message of virtue gets lost amid the regulations. The University of Michigan once attempted to suppress all speech that gave offense "on the basis of race, ethnicity, religion, national origin, sex, sexual orientation, creed, ancestry, age, marital status, handicap or Vietnam-era veteran status." The University of Connecticut felt empowered to invoke sanctions against students who engaged in "inappropriately directed laughter." Definitions can be tricky. I once heard a lawyer at a community meeting attempt to propose a resolution on group housing that would not be perceived as antihomosexual. He described an acceptable resident as "An adult person and his or her spouse or such person acting substantially in the capacity of spouse . . ." Before he could get any further, a man in the back asked, "How can we tell?"

A law enforcement officer once told of attending a drug conference in Amsterdam, in a city and a country in which drugs are easy to obtain without legal sanctions. At the end of one day's session the officer cheerfully said to a group of Dutch officials, "Let's go get some pot." The reaction: "They looked at me as though I had said, 'Let's go get laid.' "

In this place where marijuana can be easily found at youth centers and coffeehouses, the message was that it just wasn't done, which may help explain why teenagers in the Netherlands use pot far less often than their American counterparts.

It is not that the law does not have an important role; it is just that other things do as well. Such as the sort of social sanction experienced in Amsterdam by the American police officer. Or the technique used by nurses at a Missouri hospital who were being harassed by male doctors. They started sending a secret code on the PA to round up their colleagues, who would then confront the offender en masse. A similar technique has been used by cabdrivers in trouble. Upon hearing a coded radio message, all nearby taxi drivers rush to the scene.

Positive reinforcement is another alternative. If an end to discrimination, cleaning up pollution, and workplace safety are worthy social goals, then it is reasonable to reward firms that excel in reaching these goals. These rewards could be tangible (as in a tax break or public contract preference), but even public recognition (such as an official logo to use in advertising) could help. FDR thought so, and he used such recognition effectively to encourage corporate cooperation during the Depression and World War II. Most restaurateurs think so; that is why they frame and prominently post any strongly favorable reviews.

We also need to pay attention to accidental casualties of worthy efforts. The person who loses out simply because of a minority preference is sometimes viewed as a racist. It would be much healthier to recognize the contribution made to the greater good in some way, such as putting this person at the top of the next promotion list. The failure to take such matters seriously has contributed to the great anecdotal aresenal used so effectively against progressive programs in recent years.

Above all, we need to learn—or relearn—how to settle disputes in a different manner. In the early 19th century the nearly 100 residents of Maine's Monhegan Island not only got along without lawyers but didn't even have any government. According to an early island history, they handled their affairs using "certain prudential rules and usages which they had mutually established." Today even couples deeply in love are told they cannot govern themselves without a lawyer-drafted prenuptial agreement.

In the 18th century the County of Philadelphia had an official peacemaker "to prevent law suits, act in the manner of arbitrator and end strife." And before the Soviet Union and the United States got involved in Somalia, tribal chieftains sometimes settled disputes by going under a tree and not leaving until an agreement had been reached. We and the Soviets then came up with an alternative form of dispute resolution—which is to say, competing arms shipments—and nobody went under the tree anymore. Something similar has happened to our domestic society: We have forgotten how to sit under the tree; instead we call our lawyers.

To some, the mention of such precedents may seem naive and nostalgic. But when I told a professional mediator about the Somalian chiefs, she said, "That's exactly what I tell my clients. I say, 'I'll guarantee a settlement as long as nobody leaves.' " Lyndon Johnson—never considered a wuss—was known to keep parties to a labor dispute holed up at the White House until they had come to a settlement. And the Dayton accords that dramatically eased the Bosnian crisis were achieved in part because all parties promised not only to keep talking until agreement was reached but to restrict themselves to the air base where the discussions would be held.

The problem with excessive reliance on the law is that without unsupervised, unrecorded, unlitigated trust being at the core of our relationships with others, there is little possibility that together we can create anything that works well at all—no matter what it says on paper or how many judges and attorneys we have to determine what the words on paper really mean.

We can start to reinvigorate trust by using and learning alternative dispute resolution techniques, such as mediation and arbitration. The typical lawsuit is constructed on denial; both sides are encouraged to conceal the weaknesses of their cases. The remedy is typically punitive, with little attention to whether it is also corrective. In mediation and arbitration attention is directed toward solving the problem instead of just assigning blame for it. Further, such alternative approaches often handle complexity better. For example, sexual harassment cases don't happen in vacuums. Typically they are symptoms of an endemic problem. Rather than deal solely with recompense for an individual victim, an arbitrated or mediated settlement can direct itself to the environment that led to the case in question.

We can also act personally. When a problem arises, we can seek non-lawyerly, nonadversarial solutions. We can propose compromises, even when we believe we are the damaged party. We can seek restitution rather than retribution. We can teach children nonviolent means of solving their problems. We can avoid saying, every time something goes wrong, "There ought to be a law." We can, together and without legal action, begin to re-create an environment of fairness, trust, and accommodation that is essential to a happy, functioning community and country.

An American Parts List

45 million cooking and wine books sold in 1994

113,000 toll-free numbers assigned in one week in 1995

6 million Muslims, including 2,000 in
and around Des Moines

13 million people who live in trailers

292,277 overnight stays by RVs in Yellowstone Park
during the summer of 1994

10. How to find things out

(despite the media and other obstacles)

Why finding things out is so hard

1. THERE ARE TOO MANY MESSAGES.

Here's a little experiment you can try. (Please don't attempt this if you are not in good physical and mental health):

> Go around your house and turn on every device that emits a sound: radio, TV, CD player, alarm clock, stove timer, whatever. Make sure the volume is such that you can hear each device from some central location, say, your front hall or kitchen. Gather your spouse, partner, housemates and/or children at this location, and ask them to sing, play an instrument, or declaim with some force. If your dog will join in, so much the better. Now sit down and try to read a book.

You have just demonstrated in the privacy of your own home a central problem of modern media: too much data, not enough comprehension.

Every day we are bombarded with hundreds of symbols, most of

> **JOURNALISM**
>
> A profession whose business is to explain to others what it really does not understand.
> —Lord Northcliffe

I AM NEWS; THEREFORE I AM

A public high school teacher tells of one of her students from a poor neighborhood who was raped. A story about the assault appeared in the newspaper. The student brought the clipping to school and posted it on the bulletin board. It was, the teacher noted, the first time the student had received any recognition.

which register only subconsciously. In fact, the essence of contemporary media is that we are often not aware of it. What we recognize as the media—the TV, the newspaper, and so forth—represents just a fraction of the symbols and messages reaching our minds.

Marshall McLuhan put it this way to *Wired* magazine: "The real message of media today is ubiquity. It is no longer something we do, but something we are part of. It confronts us as if from the outside with all the sensory experience of the history of humanity."

The semiotician Marshall Blonsky calls it a semiosphere, "a dense atmosphere of signs triumphantly permeating all social, political and imaginative life and, arguably, constituting our desiring selves as such." McLuhan concludes that perhaps the product has become simply an enticement to get us to purchase the advertising.

2. THERE'S TOO LITTLE NEWS.

While the media may be ubiquitous, the news we want and need is hard to find. For example, the Rocky Mountain Media Watch analyzed the news content of some 100 news shows around the country on one evening and found that news about things other than war, disasters, and crime amounted to what could be typed on four double-spaced sheets of paper. Some 70 per-

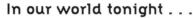

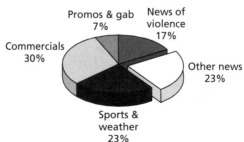

In our world tonight . . .

Promos & gab 7%
News of violence 17%
Commercials 30%
Other news 23%
Sports & weather 23%

cent of the programs, for example, featured the latest of 200 California earthquakes that month—with no injuries and little damage.

3. THE CAMERA LOOKS ONLY ONE WAY.

As our eye on the news the television camera suffers from some inherent flaws, the biggest one being that it can look only one way. If a story is happening in several or many places at once, TV will see only a little

> Fifty years ago there were about 400 cities with at least two daily papers. Today there are only 24.

piece of it. It is ill prepared to tell us about social trends, nonvisual events, or highly dispersed activities (such as a guerrilla war or multiple election campaigns).

Further, it forces news to bend to its technological needs. For example, TV finds the White House easier on its eye than is Congress with its 535 members. Thus it has contributed to the concentration of power in the presidency simply by which way it has pointed the camera. TV shows what's easy for it to see and not what's important for us to know.

4. TOO MANY JOURNALISTS ARE TOO CLOSE TO THEIR SOURCES.

In Washington especially, journalists quickly adopt the same outlook on politics and problems as those they are covering. Washington reporters have been described as people who sit around waiting for some official to lie to them. Russell Baker says that when he was a Washington correspondent, he felt like "a megaphone for the convenience of frauds."

> Typical TV sound bite during 1968 presidential campaign: 42.3 seconds
>
> During 1988 campaign: 9.8 seconds
>
> During 1992 campaign: 7.3 seconds

Instead of being an amplifier for those in power, the journalist should be the surrogate eyes and ears for those who aren't. But the cozy style of the capital has thoroughly tamed much of the press corps. Washington journalists often become members of the court rather than its observers and critics.

Many in fact are proud of their proximity to power. For example, *Washington Post* columnist Richard Harwood, in describing the Council on Foreign Relations as "the nearest thing to a ruling establishment in America,"

> We have it on his own testimony that Bill Bennett is a moral man.
> Thus Paul Farhi of the *Washington Post* found it interesting that
> Bennett's book *The Book of Virtues* should be published by Simon &
> Schuster, which is owned by Viacom, which also owns MTV,
> "scourge of conservatives everywhere." The book was a selection of
> the Book-of-the-Month Club, which is owned by Time Warner, which
> gave us Oliver Stone's *Natural Born Killers* and Ice-T's *Cop Killer*. A
> cartoon version of the book was being animated by a division of Ru-
> pert Murdoch's News Corporation, which also "peddles bare-
> breasted women in its British tabloids and racy sitcoms on its Fox
> network."

noted that 10 percent of its members were journalists. Said Harwood smugly, this is an "acknowledgment of their active and important role in public affairs and of their ascension into the American ruling class. They do not merely analyze and interpret foreign policy for the United States; they help make it."

5. TOO FEW PEOPLE DECIDE WHAT'S NEWS.

It may not be long before we find ourselves in the situation of Australia, where two thirds of the newspaper readership is controlled by one man, Rupert Murdoch. Or Britain, where Murdoch controls over one third of the newspaper readership as well as the national satellite broadcasting system (the equivalent of our entire cable system).

By the 1980s most of what Americans saw, read, or heard was controlled by fewer than two dozen corporations. By the 1990s just five corporations controlled all or part of the following cable channels: Discovery, Startz!, Encore, Learning Channel, Family Channel, Lifetime, ESPN, A&E, Disney, QVC, Cinemax, Cartoon Network, CNN, TBS, TNT, HBO, Home Shopping Network, Black Entertainment Television, Court TV, Bravo, American Movie Classics, CNBC, The Movie Channel, Comedy Central, USA Networks, MTV, Showtime, and VH1. Some 75 percent of all dailies are now in the hands of chains. In fact, just four of these chains own 21 percent of all the country's daily papers.

> Interest on Time Warner's $15 billion debt—created in part by its media investments—is $90,000 per hour.

This concentration of power has not occurred by accident, nor is it the result of economic predestination; it is not an outward sign of inner capitalist grace. Rather it is in no small part the result of a major

> Journalism consists in buying white paper at two cents a pound and selling it at ten cents a pound.
> —Charles A. Dana

dismantling of antitrust enforcement and the capitulation of the Federal Communications Commission.

6. NEWS IS JUST ANOTHER PRODUCT.

With the media increasingly part of huge conglomerates, journalism is now much more the product of corporate employees acting as reporters than it is of reporters who happen to be working for corporations.

When I started out in journalism in the 1950s, the typical reporter had only a high school education and was, by class and inclination, far more likely to side with the reader than with the boss. While some reporters were in the pockets of politicians or the mob, the consensus was that the best way to look at a government official was down your nose.

In the seventies and eighties the trade (as it had been considered) was transformed into a "profession." Aspiring journalists were expected to go to grad schools; reporters started being cited in cultural and society coverage (thus granting themselves equal status with newsmakers and other elites). Newspaper Guild locals found their members considering themselves too good for unions, and publishers began spending excessive time discussing ethics and principles, a sure sign of trouble.

HOW PAPERS USED TO COMPETE

Journalist Christopher Hitchens tells the story of the *London Daily Express* correspondent who wired home from a foreign hot spot, "*Daily Mail* man shot." His editor wired back, "Why you unshot?"

Some publishers even employed ombudsmen, purportedly to serve as the readers' advocates within the firms. These ombudsmen heard the papers' confessions and lent an aura of morality to the enterprises. Yet while the ombudsmen—like the hireling priests of the old nobility—

often provided speedy absolution, truth and the readers were not as well served. A column of polite self-criticism hardly substituted for having a second paper in town breathing down your neck.

Such shifts have not gone unnoticed by the public. A 1995

NBC/*Wall Street Journal* poll found only 26 percent of respondents having a positive or somewhat positive impression of news media; 50 percent had a negative impression. Twenty years ago a similar poll produced almost the reverse results.

Over the last century America has lost about 16 dailies annually. But in recent years this has no longer meant merely the purchase of the weaker paper in town by the stronger one. Rather nonlocal monopolies began buying up local papers, print media monopolies began buying broadcast media, local daily newspaper monopolies began buying up local weeklies, and big media monopolies began buying up small media monopolies. The journalist who wants to complain to the boss might now have to travel 2,000 miles. More important, the reporter's workplace is no longer really a newsroom as much as a corporate office.

Thus in just a few decades the American journalist has been transformed from an idiosyncratic and independent-minded member of a trade to a carefully shaped corporate employee. Some reporters aren't even called reporters; they are "team members." At the *Winston-Salem Journal,* consultants told reporters just how much time they could spend covering different categories of stories. According to a media journal, these consultants ruled that "An A-1 story should be six inches or less. A reporter should use a press release and/or one or two 'cooperative sources.' He or she should take 0.9 hours to do each story and should be able to produce 40 of these in a week." The articles reporters write and the content of the papers for which they work inevitably reflect these shifts.

7. THERE'S TOO LITTLE HISTORY IN THE NEWS.

Arthur Schlesinger, Jr., says that a community without history is like a person without a memory. The media are not particularly interested in, or knowledgeable about, history, and little of it informs news reporting. It really does help to know what happened the last time anyone tried something, but it's a question the media find singularly uninteresting.

Of course, history often turns out to be more complicated than we would like. For example, Thomas Jefferson, who is quoted approvingly several times in this book, was a slaveowner. This, in the view of some, is enough to warrant removal of his words. The assumption of such arguments is that Jefferson, unlike ourselves, would have learned nothing if he had the benefit of 200 additional years of history behind him. This strikes me as a form of aerobicism, the hubris of the living toward the departed. A more serious version of this vainglory, however, is found in the media, which all too rarely acknowledge that the past has occurred at all.

8. NUMBERS ARE USED AS ADJECTIVES; FACTS AS FILLERS.

Unlike history, facts and numbers are often mentioned in the media. The problem is that they are frequently wrong or given distorted meaning. For example, many Americans are unaware that when the press talks about a budgetary cut, it may not be an actual cut at all but only a change in relation to an imaginary baseline or projection created by some government agency. Thus a Clinton aide could go on *Meet the Press* and with a straight face say that "growing" Medicaid at 3 percent between 1995 and 2002 "is equivalent to a 38 percent reduction in spending." As Peter Carlson explained in the *Washington Post,* the 3 percent was an absolute growth, while the "cut" was relative to

> **POSTMODERN JOURNALISM**
>
> Editorial and advertising have traditionally coexisted as two distinct operations within a publishing organization, each residing on their own side of the proverbial Chinese Wall. In today's highly competitive environment, however, all publishing departments must learn how to work together to maintain the quality and profitability of the publication.
> —Announcement for a seminar organized by *Folio: The Magazine for Magazine Management*

projections of expenditures if current annual growth continued. Got it?

Polls can also create problems. A *U.S. News & World Report* article, for example, noted that answers to an inquiry about abortion varied markedly depending on whether it was asked by a man or a woman, and a question about blacks varied depending on whether it was asked by a white or a black. Changing the order in which things are compared made a big difference. The same words reordered within a sentence changed the results.

Further, the underlying facts of our politics and culture are so poorly understood that our opinions can be heavily distorted by faulty premises. For example, one poll found that nearly three quarters of Americans believe that foreign aid accounts for more than one tenth of all federal spending. It's actually less than 1 percent. Asked what would be a fair expenditure for foreign aid, the average respondent said 5 percent. Thus many misinformed voters favored cutting foreign aid even though it was only one fifth of what they considered reasonable.

Similarly, only half of those surveyed in 1995 could name Newt Gingrich as Speaker of the House, and whites think there are twice as many blacks, Latinos, and Asians in the country as is actually the case. This sort of misunderstanding of basic facts can lead to some pretty terrible politics and policy.

9. THERE ARE TOO MANY PEOPLE LYING TO YOU.

The ability of people to lie to you through the media has grown enor-

A journalist is a man who has missed his calling.

—Bismarck

mously. The average large corporation and its advertising agencies, lobbyists, and PR flacks have more manipulative skills at their disposal than the entire Nazi propaganda machine. The same is true of the White House or major political campaigns. Between advertising and politics you're probably hearing more lies, exaggerations, and distortions in a single day than you would hear during a full season at a

AND NOW HERE'S PETER JENNINGS WITH THE EVENING WORD CHOICE

Anchor consultant Susan Peterson told the *Washington Post* that when we communicate, body language counts for 55 percent of the message that gets through. "Voice tone is 38 percent. The two of those create trust. Finally, you get word choice, at 7 percent."

Minnesota fishing camp. Not only do the disinformation, misinformation, spin, and hype foul our internal data banks, but they make us far more cynical and suspicious than is healthy.

What can we do about it? One thing is to borrow a principle from financial investing: Diversify. The more (and more varied) sources of information you have, the less likely you'll be led astray. This is one reason that I subscribe to both the liberal *Nation* and the conservative *Insight*.

10. AND THEN THERE'S TV.

Polls tell us that nearly a majority of Americans say they get *all* their news from television and that three quarters say they get *most* of their news from the tube.

It is difficult to overstate the importance of TV not just because of its prominence but because of its effects as well. TV is a cool medium. Watch C-SPAN and notice how physically quiet the guests are. They rarely gesticulate; they do not bob and weave. Instead they sit much like those watching, albeit upright rather than sprawled (and without the potato chips). Guest or viewer, TV encourages stillness. It seldom inspires us to engage in any social or civic activity. Instead it encourages those on either side of the screen just to stay where they are and keep looking straight ahead.

TV does not come close to meeting Mark Twain's standard for a good newspaper: that it should not

> TVs just go by themselves.
> —A six-year-old explaining
> to Phil Donahue the advantage
> of computers over television

only print the news but make us mad enough to do something about it. But here are a few of the things it may very well do to you:

- It can make you afraid when you don't have to be.
- It can get you to buy things you don't need.
- It can waste your time.
- It can make you feel life is too complicated to change.
- It warns you against things you'll never run into but doesn't give much useful guidance about those you will.
- It can make you passive and docile.
- It can tell you in an authoritative voice things that are not true.
- It can make you, your family, and your community seem insignificant.
- It can keep you inside on a beautiful day.

Eight ways the news gets corporatized

1. There is now only one daily in most American cities. Stories can be ignored without fear that the competition will run them.

2. The labor beat, once an important assignment in major print media, has been eliminated. Workers are now primarily covered as consumers, not as employees.

> Newspapers are unable, seemingly, to discriminate between a bicycle accident and the collapse of civilization.
>
> —G. B. Shaw

3. Important stories are hidden in the business or real estate sections.

4. There is poor coverage of environmental and worker safety stories that might adversely impact on corporations and advertisers.

5. There is heavy editorial support for public policies favoring local business interests, such as subsidized downtown development, sports arenas, etc. News about citizen criticism of such projects is often suppressed.

6. Media tend to defend their local industries more than their local communities. Headlines read BIGGO TRIMS 4,000 JOBS rather than BIGGO FIRES 4,000 or 4,000 FAMILIES DISRUPTED BY BIGGO LAYOFFS.

7. Big media are more reliant on big advertisers and more vulnerable to boycotts by these advertisers. Newt Gingrich has urged just such boycotts, calculating that the twenty biggest advertisers could effectively silence opposing views.

8. There is an emphasis on indicators that are of interest to corporations (such as productivity, GDP, etc.) instead of those of interest to workers (such as real wages, housing prices, etc.)

How you can use the media

THINK OF MEDIA AS A STREAM.

The first rule of media survival is use it; don't let it use you. We must ignore the role the media has prescribed for us—audience, consumer, addict—and treat it much as the trout treats a stream, a medium in which to swim and not to drown.

The trick is to stop the media from happening *to* you and to treat it as an environment, a carrier. Then you can cease being a consumer or a victim and become a hunter and a gatherer, foraging for signs that are good and messages that are important and data you can use. Then the zapper and the mouse become tools and weapons and not addictions. Then you turn off the TV not because it is evil but because you have gotten whatever it has to offer and now must look somewhere else.

FLY UNDER THE RADAR.

There is a vast and frequent exchange of information and thoughts flying beneath the radar of conventional media. For example, a strong and vital community will have a powerful information flow. In some ways the Internet simply replicates the transmission of data in a healthy community. Information is sent out in many different directions with a redundancy and inefficiency that assure an efficient result: The data will actually be received. News may be transferred at church, at the barbershop, between extended family members, or on the corner. The more casual conversation there is in a culture, the more news can be transmitted.

> Public television's most famous news show, *The Newshour with Jim Lehrer,* is two thirds owned by the conservative media conglomerate TCI. Nearly half the program budget for 1995, reports the media watchdog FAIR, came from two politically active firms: the agribusiness giant Archer Daniels Midland and the New York Life Insurance Company.

LEARN TO NARROWCAST.

In fact, the mass media is often not the best way to get your message out. As a general rule, the more people your message reaches, the less impact it will have on each one. There are several reasons for this:

- ☞ Mass media encourages consumption rather than action.
- ☞ Those who respond to your message will be small compared with all the couch potatoes who won't. A lot of your energy and/or money will be wasted.
- ☞ In order to reach a mass audience you have to tone down, modify, or censor your message. In effect you will have to destroy some of what you are trying to transmit.

Those involved in political campaigns and lobbying understand such phenomena with scary precision. They call it narrowcasting. Someone is narrowcasting to you all the time— from the ads in your hobby or sports magazine to direct mail that comes to your house every day. Mail campaigns can be tailored for specific ethnic or geographical groups in a way a TV ad never could.

There are even elaborate propaganda factories designing pseudo-grassroots—or AstroTurf—campaigns to pressure members of Congress with carefully orchestrated "personal" phone calls.

The AstroTurf experts—with all the mass media at their command— have effectively concluded that when you come right down to it, it's hard to beat the sound of the human voice saying what it thinks. It turns out that television didn't replace all of us after all.

DO IT ON THE NET.

For those seeking alternatives to the mass media, the Internet is the most phenomenal new medium of our times. Here, after all, is a system so

> Children—whether white, black, or Latino—use computers far more than adults, according to a 1993 Census Bureau poll. For example, 46 percent of black and Latino children use computers, but only 38 percent of white adults.
>
> According to another poll, about 20 percent of those 18 to 25 access the Web, but only 3 percent of those over 50.

well designed by the Defense Department to prevent its destruction that now even the Defense Department can't destroy it.

The political and social potential of the Internet has largely been an act of individual discovery by millions of individuals, thousands of organizations, and a relatively few imaginative theorists and dreamers.

> At some point, technology might allow us to provide each of our readers with a customized product. We will be able to send one person an editorial backing one position and the next person will receive one that is just the opposite.
>
> —Randy Cope, publisher of the *Northwest Arkansas Times*

The conventional media and politicians have also expressed great interest and concern, but as in so many matters, their interest and that of the public are far apart. Thus there has been considerable political and media angst concerning sex on the Internet, although on the Net itself users of all sorts have taken the existence of sex quite in stride.

The real concerns about the Net reflect less a worry over morals than a fear of competition. While both conventional and cable television posed commercial threats to the print media, the Internet does even more: it reduces the need for any centralized sources of information. With the Net, citizens no longer have to rely on the clichés of underinformed and overinflated correspondents.

There is of course considerable potential for individual users or the government to spread false information. The Net is for the most part, however, a propagandist's nightmare. Unlike swastikas on the wall, hate mail, obscene phone calls, or White House spin for that matter, the lie often does not fester long before it is revealed as such by other users. The truth may be only a few hours or messages away. The effect is often like being able to read in your morning paper letters complaining about articles in the same issue.

> One of the by-products of the Internet has been an explosion of hype about the Internet. It may help to keep this all in perspective to realize that the number of Net users in this country is still fewer than the number of those already watching TV in the mid-1950s.

The Internet and democracy

- ☞ The Internet is the most powerful and least expensive new media tool for the preservation and propagation of democracy.
- ☞ Corporations, large media, intelligence agencies, and politicians

> As I was working on this chapter, I received a chain e-mail from Stevie and Amanda, two young students in Massachusetts who were doing a science project on the Internet and wanted to see how many people would reply to their message. One day later I received an e-mail from "Stevie's Mom & Dad" begging that no more replies be sent. They were coming in at a rate of eight a minute.

know this and are working overtime to figure out how to bring it under control. Their interest in censorship is part of a larger effort to control access to, and use of, the Net.

☞ Information about the Net from sources such as the megamedia is deeply suspect since they have a vital economic interest in altering it. To stay abreast of issues concerning the Net, follow information in nonconglomerated computer publications or on the Web sites of computer information freedom groups. In other words, trust your mouse and not the Mouse.

☞ One of the best assets of the Internet is that its advocates tend to be smarter than its exploiters. Within hours of Congress's proposing an onerous censorship measure, people were busy creating a new program to get round it.

☞ You are never too old to learn how to use e-mail, the Net news groups, and the Web. Stop saying so, and get your kid to explain it to you. Or take a course.

☞ You are never too poor to demand access to the Net. Instead of saying things like "Well, the Internet is just for the elite," demand that your library, schools, and other public facilities provide terminals and training. The success of the Net as a democratic catalyst will depend in no small part on the principle of computer access as a human right.

☞ Insist that all essential local, state, and federal government information be available at Web sites. Oppose all attempts to privatize public information by contracting out archives to corporations.

☞ Resist all attempts to censor the Net. There will be plenty.

☞ There's a lot of rumor, hyperbole, disinformation, and ignorance on the Net Treat information from unknown cybersources with the same skepticism you'd give someone on the street trying to sell you a gold watch just pulled from his pocket.

☞ The Net is a community as well as a medium. The same rules apply as in any healthy community. These include not boring other people to death, not screaming, and letting others have their say. We shouldn't take advantage of others' time by trying to sell them something they didn't inquire about. And if someone abuses the community by, say, using ethnic epithets, we should handle the problem within the community and not resort to the FBI or congressional legislation.

✏ Remember the great lesson of the Internet: We can have fun, provide and find information, and help one another without *anyone* being in charge. Borrow this lesson from the Internet, and apply it in your own community.

24 cheap & easy ways to make your own media

FOR COUCH POTATOES

1. **Get a Web site.** It isn't hard. Just think of it as a great big silent fax machine that doesn't tie up your phone.

2. **Change your media habits—regularly.** We all fall into habits of reading and watching. Shake them up periodically. Drop the subscription to that magazine you hardly read anymore, and replace it with a cheap introductory offer to something new. If you live in a city, visit the best newsstand in town, and spend some time browsing through the publications there. If you find one you like, buy it and subscribe. Look at one new TV program a week. Watch Spanish-language TV for a few minutes even if you don't speak Spanish. Hang out in bookstores. Turn on a radio station aimed at people who don't agree with you.* Read a columnist you hate, and argue with the points made in the column. Check out public access television. Watch a televangelist, and try to figure out why he's affecting millions and you aren't.

3. **Write a letter to an editor.** Editors get far fewer letters than you might think. Some have even been known to write their own. Keep yours short; a few paragraphs are enough. Make a new point; don't just vent your spleen. Localize a national issue—i.e., show how national welfare cuts can't be replaced by the social programs of churches like yours. If you can't be funny, *New Yorker* editor Harold Ross said, then be interesting.

*I even listen to Rush sometimes while I'm out doing Saturday errands and I haven't had an accident yet.

And sign just one name to it. Editors look at multiple signatures as a form of gang assault.

4. **Read the jump page.** It's one of the places newspapers hide the news.

5. **Write a politician.** While it is true that most politicians don't read letters, they have people who do. The president gets 40,000 to 60,000 letters a week (and about 10,000 e-mail messages) and will read about 10 or 15. But the president and his staff have a good idea of how these letters are going. Add yours to the pile. E-mail is an easy way of doing it these days. When Congress was talking about legislation to spy on electronic transmissions, the cybercommunity produced over 40,000 names on an e-mail petition opposing this move. When President Clinton was presented with a bill mandating major wilderness timber cutting, he received 13,500 e-mails and 8,000 phone calls—along with 600 pieces of wood.

6. **Call a politician.** Even the president only receives about 2,000 calls a day on his comment line. Senators and city council members get far fewer. You won't be able to speak to the president and you may not be able to speak to the council member, but you can always leave a message. A good time to schedule calls to a politician is during lunch. There are fewer people in the office, so a handful of calls may seem like a lot. The pros figure that each call to a Congress member represents the views of 200 to 400 voters.

7. **Ask someone, "What's happenin'?"** Remember what Blanche Dubois said in *A Streetcar Named Desire*: "I have always relied on the kindness of strangers." Our culture increasingly discourages contact with strangers—even among adults. This makes us more suspicious of one another and denies us the knowledge that casual contact can bring.

8. **Call a talk show.** One of the best-kept secrets is how often people *don't* call talk shows. If you notice the host giving out the station number more frequently than usual, it may be because business is slow. Some times of day are easier to get on than others. For example, 11:00 P.M. is when many people desert their radios for TV news. If the show is really popular, start dialing even before it's on the air. If a representative of your group is going to be on, make sure members of the group call to ask friendly questions. And don't be afraid to call shows that emphasize a viewpoint opposed to your own. Don't cede the airwaves to the other side. As 20/20 Vision points out in its guide to talk shows, "Research has shown that the listening audience for this medium is remarkably nonideological and, in fact, tunes in just to hear a diversity of opinion."

9. **Watch historical documentaries on cable, or read a book about the past.** The more you know about the past, the less you'll be fooled about the present. Take something that interests you, such as a hobby or an event, and find out its history. Along the way you'll learn a lot of other things as well.

FOR THE ACTIVE

10. **Don't play spin doctor.** The prime rule of public relations is to do it right the first time: If you are ineffective, disorganized, misinformed, or just plain wrong, don't expect PR to dig you out of your hole. Get your own act together before telling others about it.

11. **Use a fax machine.** Fax machines that will semiautomatically broadcast to over 100 locations are now available. Computer fax programs will handle many times more. This means your group can fax to the most important locations in town (the mayor, council, media, other groups) on a regular basis. You can reach even more with a fax tree: get others to rebroadcast your fax to their own lists. Keep the fax short and punchy. Remember, scissors cut paper, and frequency beats length. The Rainbow Coalition puts out a regular and effective fax that's just one page long.

12. **Use radio.** So the local daily won't cover your organization or story? Stop worrying about it. It'd probably give you only a paragraph or two at best. Go where the people are: listening to the radio. According to the Radio Advertising Bureau, "Americans average about three hours of radio listening per day. Two out of three Americans are listening to the radio during prime time and radio is the first morning news source for most people." Because radio is so taken for granted, the skill and potential involved in using it well are often discounted. Tony Schwartz, a guru in guerrilla media circles, says that the protest movements of the sixties would have been far more successful if they had put more of their money into radio and less into marches and demonstrations. Schwartz is a strong advocate of well-produced radio spots. He knows they work. Sometimes you don't even have to broadcast the spot. When the city council was considering a bill to which he was opposed, for example, Schwartz made two professionally produced spot announcements. One of the spots praised the council members for voting down the bill. The other excoriated them for approving it. Schwartz sent both spots to each

member of the council with a letter saying he wanted their advice on which spot he should run. The measure was voted down.

13. **Buy time on radio.** It is often cheaper than you think, especially if you are careful to target your message to the right station. You can buy blocks of time at off-peak hours and create your own radio program. Though it may be a minor station, if those who support your cause know where to find you, you will be able to reach them. Ethnic and religious groups have been using buy-your-own-programming for years, sometimes supported solely by listener contributions.

14. **Start a neighborhood newsletter.** It doesn't have to be elaborate. Two sides of a 8 1/2 by 11 sheet will be fine (or you can go to a speedy print and do a full four-page newsletter). Start out small. In every neighborhood only a minority of people become actively involved. Aim for these people. When I was a neighborhood commissioner, with 2,000 residents in my district, I came up with a list of about 200 addresses of active people. I included people who had come to commission meetings, called me, or had signed petitions. I personally delivered the newsletter on a Saturday, leaving extra copies at the public school and library. I also asked people to contribute a small amount to help keep it going. I met lots of constituents this way, got ideas, heard lots of complaints, and received some compliments too.

15. **Use public access TV.** Find someone with TV or video skills, and make use of these public channels. Be careful, though. Third-generation amateur videos can make your cause look like an exhibit at a poorly maintained aquarium.

16. **Join or start a study circle or salon.** Study circles began in Scandinavia but are becoming increasingly popular here. The idea is for neighbors and friends to study a current issue and then come together to discuss it. Salons are informal gatherings of people with common interests. They can be organized as a meeting, party, or potluck supper. The idea in its contemporary form has received a big boost from *Utne Reader* magazine. National and local newsletters and Web pages about the salon movement are available. One idea would be to organize a regular gathering to which each member would bring something of importance learned since the last meeting. It might be a news story, but it might just as easily be a poem or a moving tale about some member of the community. Together these contributions would make up a living newspaper.

17. **Visit editors.** Ordinary citizens and their organizations are far too humble in dealing with newspaper editors and broadcast news directors. Get some groups or churches together, and request a meeting to discuss your concerns. If you have a specific agenda, lay it out. Suggest how coverage of these concerns could be improved.

18. **Take a reporter out to lunch.** Despite their pretenses to the contrary, reporters are human beings too. Treat them that way, and it'll start to wear down the professional pose they frequently assume. Often reporters have to be educated about the importance of an issue. It's easier to do over a drink than over a deadline. Take your time. Build trust. Be friendly and not didactic. Best of all, become a source; reporters always protect their sources.

19. **Teach kids about advertising and propaganda.** Nothing we teach them is more important than giving them spiel immunity at an early age. Besides, you can deconstruct the ads they come across and teach them reading at the same time. You can introduce them to propaganda's effects and run a concurrent course on statistics. Of course, you have to be prepared to have them actually enjoy class.

20. **Build an e-mail list.** Send out news and information to a list of friends, members, politicians and the media.*

21. **Hold a meeting.** It still works amazingly well.

22. **Use news releases and news conferences but not too often.** These are highly overrated media tools. Thousands of acres of trees have died to make unread news releases. Still, they are useful for event announcements (reporters like to have something printed in order to double-check times and spellings) and complicated stories (such as in science and medicine) that need precise wording. Here are a few not-so-good ideas: telling people about an event that took place last week, deadly analyses of not-too-interesting issues, a boring news bite hidden in an wordy release. Keep it short, keep it interesting, and if you can't find a strong news peg to put in the first sentence, don't send it.

23. **Stay out of the media until you're ready.** Don't assume that all publicity is good publicity. For example, is your effort strong enough to withstand dismissive and disparaging treatment by the media? Do you have only a 12-hour revolution, launched with a news conference at 11:00 A.M. and last heard from on the 11:00 P.M. news? Or do you have

*It's a good idea to make sure your friends want to be on the list. Offer in each message the chance to remove themselves from the list by sending a reply with the word *unsubscribe*.

something solid that will continue to build with or without the mass media's help?

24. **Use the telephone.** One of the most effective activists I ever knew was the late civil rights leader Julius Hobson. Julius used to claim that he could start a revolution with six people and a telephone booth. Since six people and a telephone booth are often all you've got, it's not a bad trick to learn.

An American Parts List

464,000 children in foster homes

300 million pounds of pepperoni
annually to put on pizza

450 million pages of government classified material
waiting to be reviewed for declassification

1 million Americans sick each
year from bad drinking water

400 million animals turned into road kill each year,
including 56,000 deer hit by cars in Michigan

112 million Americans who could
have voted in 1994 but didn't

11. How to get along with other Americans

Living next to 250 million people who aren't quite like you

The most important fact about race

It doesn't really exist. At least not the way many Americans think it does. There is simply no undisputed scientific definition of race. What are considered genetic characteristics are often the result of cultural habit and environmental adaptation. As far back as 1785 a German philosopher noted that "complexions run into each other." Julian Huxley suggested in 1941 that "it would be highly desirable if we could banish the question-begging term 'race' from all discussions of human affairs and substitute the noncommittal phrase 'ethnic group.' That would be a first step toward rational consideration of the problem at hand." Anthropologist Ashley Montagu in 1942 called race our "most dangerous myth."

Yet in our conversations and arguments, in our media, and even in our laws, the illusion of race is given great credibility. As a result, that which is transmitted culturally is considered genetically fixed, that which is an environmental adaptation is regarded as innate and that which is fluid is declared immutable.

Many still hang on to a notion similar to that of Carolus Linnaeus, who declared in 1758 that there were four races: white, red, dark, and black. Others make up their own races, applying the term to religions (Jewish), language groups (Aryan), or nationalities (Irish). Modern science has little impact on our views. Our concept of race comes largely from religion, literature, politics, and the oral tradition. It comes creaking with all the prejudices of the ages. It reeks of territoriality, jingoism, subjugation, and the abuse of power.

DNA research has revealed just how great is our misconception of race. In *The History and Geography of Human Genes*, Luca Cavalli-Sforza of Stanford and his colleagues describe how many of the variations between humans are really adaptations to different environmental conditions (such as the relative density of sweat glands or having lean bodies to dissipate heat and fat ones to retain it). But that's not the sort of thing you can easily build a system of apartheid around. As Thomas S. Martin has written, "The widest genetic divergence in human groups separates the Africans from the Australian aborigines, though ironically these two 'races' have the same skin color . . . There is no clearly distinguishable 'white race.' What Cavalli-Sforza calls the Caucasoids are a hybrid, about two-thirds Mongoloid and one-third African. Finns and Hungarians are slightly more Mongoloid, while Italians and Spaniards are more African, but the deviation is vanishingly slight."

A guide to some new races

If we are going to insist on dividing people by race, we should at least use comparisons more up-to-date than those thought up centuries ago. Here are a few suggestions based on modern science:

Basis of comparison	New races
Blood type	The New Guinean–Germans
	The Japanese-Estonians
	The Celtic-Indians
Front teeth	The Swedish-Indians
Ability to digest milk	The Norwegian-Arab-Nigerians
Nose length	The English-Algerians

Well, it sure feels like race

Regardless of what science says, however, myth can kill and cause pain just as easily as scientific truth. And regardless of what science says, there are no

Japanese players in the NBA or, as anthropologist Alice Brues told *Newsweek*, "If I parachute into Nairobi, I know I'm not in Oslo."

In fact, give or take a few thousand years, it's unlikely that those with Nordic skin complexions would stay that way living under the African sun. Similarly, the effects of a U.S. diet are strong enough that the first generations of both European and Asian Americans have found themselves looking up at their grandchildren.

In such ways adaptation mimics what many think of as race. But who needs science when we have our own eyes? If it looks like race, that's good enough for us.

Further, we are obsessed with the subject even as we say we wish to ignore it. A few years back a study of urban election coverage found five times as many stories about race as about taxes.

We can't even agree on what race is. In the 1990 census Americans said they belonged to some 300 different races or ethnic groups. American Indians divided themselves into 600 tribes, and Latinos into 70 categories.

The real reason race is important to us

Even as we talk endlessly of race and ethnicity, we simultaneously go to great lengths to prove that we are all the same. Why this contradiction? The answer can be partly found in the tacit assumption of many that human equity must be based primarily on competitive equality. Listen to talk about race (or sex) and notice how often the talk is also about competition. The cultural differences (real or presumed) that really disturb us are ones of competitive significance: thigh circumference, height, math ability, and so forth. We accept more easily other differences—varieties of hair, degree of subcutaneous fat, prevalence of sickle-cell anemia—because they don't affect (or affect far less) who gets to the top.

Once having decided which traits are important, we assign causes to them on the basis of convenience rather than fact. Our inability to sort out the relative genetic, cultural, and environmental provenance of our differences doesn't impede our judgment at all. It is enough that a difference is observed. Thus we tend to deal neither

> ## RACE AND COMPETITION
>
> The spirit of aggressive competition is inculcated in the young American [boy] almost as soon as he is capable of understanding what is required of him. He soon learns that his parents' love is conditioned upon how he compares—measures up—with others; He must compete and be successful.
>
> All potential competing persons and groups . . . come to be regarded as rivals, and inevitably they will be regarded with varying degrees of hostility and fear. . . . Race prejudice constitutes a socially sanctioned outlet for the resulting accumulated aggressiveness; this at once serves to explain the person's failure to himself and at the same time enables him to revenge himself upon the imagined cause of it.
>
> —Ashley Montagu

with understanding what the facts about our differences and similarities really mean—or, more important, with their ultimate irrelevance to developing a world where we can live harmoniously and happily with one another. We don't spend the effort to separate facts from fiction because both cut too close to our inability to appreciate and celebrate our human differences. It is far easier to pretend either that these differences are immutable or that they don't exist at all.

The Catch-22 of ethnicity

And so we come to the Catch-22 of ethnicity. It is hard to imagine a nondiscriminatory, unprejudiced society in which race and sex matter much. Yet in our efforts to reach that goal, our society and its institutions constantly send

> After two decades of progress toward integration, the separation of black children in America's schools is on the rise and is in fact approaching the levels of 1970, before the first school bus rolled at the order of a court.
>
> —James S. Kunen, *Time*

the conflicting message that they are extremely important.

For example, our laws against discriminatory practices inevitably heighten general consciousness of race and sex. The media, drawn inexorably to conflict, play up the issue. And the very groups that have suffered under racial or sexual stereotypes consciously foster countering stereotypes—"you wouldn't understand, it's a black thing"—as a form of protection. Thus we find ourselves in the odd position of attempting to create a society that shuns invidious distinctions while at the same time—often with fundamentalist or regulatory fervor—accentuating those distinctions.

In the process we reduce our ethnic problems to a matter of regulation and power and reduce our ambitions to the achievement of a tolerable stalemate rather than the creation of a truly better society. The positive aspects of diversity remain largely ignored, and nondiscrimination becomes merely another symbol of virtuous citizenship—like not double-parking or paying your taxes.

Martin Luther King said once: "Something must happen so as to touch the hearts and souls of men that they will come together, not because the law says it, but because it is natural and right."

Sorry, Martin. Our approach to prejudice and discrimination is not unlike our approach to drugs: We simply plan to rule them out of existence. In so doing, we have implicitly defined the limits of virtue as merely the absence of malice.

The most important fact about prejudice

It's normal. That isn't to say that it's nice, pretty, or desirable. Only that suspicion, distrust, and distaste for outsiders are deeply human traits. The anthropologist Ruth Benedict wrote that "all primitive tribes agree in recognizing [a] category of the outsiders, those who are not only outside the provisions of the moral code which holds within the limits of one's own people, but who are summarily denied a place anywhere in the human scheme.

A great number of the tribal names in common use, Zuñi, Déné, Kiowa . . . are only their native terms for 'the human beings,' that is, themselves. Outside of the closed group there are no human beings."

Many attempts to eradicate racism from our society have been based on the opposite notion: that those who harbor prejudice toward others are abnormal and social deviants. Further, we often describe these "deviants" only in terms of their overt antipathies: They are "anti-Semitic" or guilty of "hate." In fact, once you have determined yourself to be human and others less so, you need not hate them any more than you need despise the fish you eat for dinner. This is why those who participate in genocide can do so with such calm; they have defined their targets as outside humanity.

What if instead we were to start with the unhappy truth that humans have always had a hard time dealing with other peoples and that much ethnic and sexual antagonism stems not from hate so much as from cultural narcissism? Then our repertoire of solutions might tilt more toward education and mediation and away from being self-righteous multicultural missionaries converting yahoos in the wilds of the soul. We could turn toward something more akin to what Andrew Young once described as a sense of "no fault justice." We might begin to consider seriously Martin Luther King's admonition to his colleagues that among their dreams should be that someday their enemies would be their friends.

Tellling stories

If we are to rid our minds of stereotypes, something needs to fill the empty space. Nothing works better than the real stories of real people drawn from the anecdotal warehouses that supply many of our deepest values, feelings, and philosophy.

If you find your classroom, organization, or workplace bogged down in cultural tension and abstract confrontation—or perhaps

---

ELUSIVE STEREOTYPE #306

[Mick Jagger] self-consciously emulated the gruff singing style of black Chicago bluesman Howlin' Wolf, who himself reputedly got his name trying to imitate the white country singer Jimmy Rodgers. Rodgers, for his part, drew on nineteenth century black traditions—and on the English culture that later produced a twentieth-century middle-class white youth like Jagger who wanted to sing like a poor black American

—Jim Cullen,
The Art of Democracy

feeling the silence that comes from being near one another and not knowing what to say—why not take a break and let people tell their own stories?

In writing this book, I sat down with a number of people who had crossed the barricades of culture to some good end. I wanted their wisdom but I also wanted their stories, for wisdom seldom comes without a tale.

If I were just to tell you that each had experienced "institutional racism" or had suffered from some sort of "cultural stereotype," you'd probably forget about it before the end of this chapter. Here instead are a few of their stories:

- ☞ KYUNG KYU LIM is employed by an association of state transportation officials in Washington, D.C. He is active with Young Koreans United and has worked in multicultural coalitions. He believes that "part of getting Korean-American identity is learning commonalities with other groups." In the early seventies Kyung Kyu moved from Korea to an African American community in L.A. In high school, through a program ironically called A Better Chance, he ended up with a white host family in suburban Minneapolis, where the overwhelmingly white student body made him feel "wretched," with its clannishness, nice cars, and derogatory comments about "boat people."

  "I felt myself shrinking," Kyung Kyu recalls.

  Things got no better at Macalester College. The prejudice he found there made him feel "smaller and smaller." He tried running away by dropping out and moving to Alaska. That didn't work. Nor did changing schools to the University of Connecticut; not long after he arrived, members of the football team spit upon some Asian students.

- ☞ RUDY ARREDONDO handles civil rights problems for the Department of Agriculture and has worked with César Chavez and for a city health department. He came to Texas from Mexico when he was 3. By 5 he was working in the fields. When he was 6, his mother put him on a bus to go to kindergarten for the first time. As he sat down, the Anglo passengers started screaming at him. He knew no English, so he did not realize that the bus was segregated and that he was in the white section. He knew only that strange people were screaming at him in a foreign tongue, and he was very scared. At 12 Rudy tried to buy a movie ticket in Lubbock. The clerk pointed to a sign that read NO NIGGERS, DOGS OR MEXICANS ALLOWED.

- ☞ JOHN CALLAHAN is editing the unpublished works of Ralph Ellison. He grew up in New Haven. At the age of 8—and a small 8—he was sent to a parochial school in the formerly-Irish-turned-Italian neighborhood of Fairhaven. There he was greeted by some seemingly friendly (and much bigger) Italian kids, who asked him, "Do you know what an Irishman is?" John said he didn't, and one of the kids said, "A nigger turned inside out." They pummeled him, and one grabbed his Yankees' baseball hat, saying of the team's star, "DiMag belongs to us."

Later, when he was 16 and working as a mail clerk for a bank, he overheard a bank officer on the phone. The bank officer was looking out the window, his long legs stretched over a corner of his desk. He was saying, "If the funny little mick doesn't work out, we can always bring in a nigger."

But Kyung Kyu, Rudy, and John also told me a different type of story. For example, Kyung Kyu remembered that at his elementary school it was black teachers who helped him through the wrenching experience of being a young stranger in a new land. They also taught him how to handle the kids who taunted him for his poor English: by saying he was Korean and proud of it.

Kyung Kyu became a community organizer and eventually found his way East and to a MIT program for organizers run by Mel King—a longtime African American activist and onetime candidate for mayor of Boston. King became his teacher and guide.

When I talked with Rudy, our conversation turned to Sammie Abdullah Abbott. Sammie, the grandson of Arab Christian immigrants who had fled Turkish persecution in Syria, was an activist who led the local antifreeway crusade in the sixties and eventually became mayor of Takoma Park, Maryland. Along the way he taught a Latino organizer and an Anglo-Irish journalist a lot about politics and life. At his memorial service I had said that for Sammie, "a cause was not a career move, not an option purchased on a political future, nor a flirtation of conscience. It was simply the just life's work of a just human." Rudy recalled that "Sam Abbott had preconceived notions about everything. We would have strong arguments." Yet when Sam became mayor, the town meetings often ran late because he "never used a gavel to shut anyone up."

Someone also crossed the barriers to help John Callahan. Going through, and dropping out of, college, John worked for two African Americans, who "taught me a great deal about the hard work of becoming a man." Later still, when Callahan had become a man and an academic, he wrote an essay about a black novelist. He sent a copy to the writer, who responded with a long letter and an offer that they get together if John ever came to New York.

That's how, just before 4:00 P.M. one day in 1978, John Callahan found himself ringing the doorbell of Ralph Ellison. "We talked like we were in a Henry James novel," says Callahan. Ellison called him Mr. Callahan, and Callahan called him Mr. Ellison. Then, at precisely five minutes to five, Ellison leaned toward Callahan and asked, "John, would you like a drink?"

"Why, yes, Mr. Elli—ah, Ralph—I would." Ellison excused himself and returned with two bottles of whiskey, one bourbon and one Irish. They began to talk again, but no longer as in a Henry James novel and only for the first of many times.

Much later Ralph Ellison told John's mother that if he and his wife had had a son, they would have liked him to have been like John. Today John Callahan is editing the unfinished works of a black author who found something of himself in an Irish kid from New Haven.

THREE REASONS WHY COLLEGES AND UNIVERSITIES MAY NOT BE SUCH GOOD PLACES TO LEARN ABOUT DIVERSITY

1. They are themselves traditional, hierarchical, and rigid cultures.
2. Two main sources of problems on campus—sports teams and fraternities—are usually exempt from real reform because of their importance to alumni fundraising.
3. Parents send their children to college to learn how to compete much more than to learn how to cooperate.

How Mr. Platt did it

In the middle of the stolid, segregated, monolithic 1950s, Howard Platt taught one of two anthropology courses available in an American high school. I was lucky enough to be among his students. Mr. Platt showed us a new way to look at the world.

And what a wonderful world it was. Not the stultifying world of our parents, not the monochromatic world of our neighborhood, not the boring world of ninth grade, but a world of fantastic options, a world in which people got to cook, eat, shelter themselves, have sex, dance, and pray in an extraordinary variety of ways. Mr. Platt's subliminal message of cultural relativism was simultaneously a subliminal message of freedom. You were not a prisoner of your culture; you could always go live with the Eskimos, the Indians, or the Arabs. By the time the bell sounded I was often ready to go.

Mr. Platt did not exorcise racism, and he did not teach ethnic harmony, cultural sensitivity, the regulation of diversity, or the morality of nonprejudiced behavior. He didn't need to. He taught something far more important, something so often missing from our discussions on race, something frequently absent from college curricula. Mr. Platt opened a world of variety, not for us to fear but to learn about, appreciate, and enjoy. It was not an obstacle but a gift.

Finding the right words

Linguists say that when something matters greatly in a culture, there are many words for it. Here in America we have no single word for a four-wheeled vehicle. Yet when dealing with issues of race and sex, we have comfortably settled on *racism* and *sexism,* two overburdened words called to fulfill an astounding collection of functions. The net effect is to dissipate the power of the most violent acts and to exaggerate minor transgressions. Linguistically we have put genocide and the failure of a professor to assign any reading by a black author on the same level.

If we were really going to do something about our problems, we would have more words for them. We would discriminate, linguistically, tactically, and philosophically, between a black saying "nigger," a white freshman using the epithet, and a white politician saying the same thing. We would be able to describe the difference between the prejudice that comes from being taught that another ethnic group is responsible for your economic problems and that which comes from believing another ethnic group is trying to take your power. We would distinguish among the misguided, the uninformed, the victim

> In the movie *Welcome to the Dollhouse,* teenager Mark Wiener explains growing up to his 11-year-old sister: "They call you names, but not as much to your face."

Before P.C.

Saul Alinsky, in *Rules for Radicals,* describes trying to organize an Indian group in Canada. The Indians argued that they couldn't organize because, as one put it, "If we organize that means getting out and fighting the way you are telling us to do and that would mean that we would be corrupted by the white man's culture and lose our own values." Alinsky asked the Indians to describe these values. "Creative fishing" was given as an example. Asked to explain, one said, "Well, to begin with, when we go out fishing, we get away from everything. We get way out in the woods." Alinsky: "Well, we whites don't exactly go fishing in Times Square, you know." Reply: "Yes, but it's different with us. When we go out, we're out on the water and you can hear the lap of the waves on the bottom of the canoe, and the birds in the trees and the leaves rustling and—you know what I mean?" Alinsky: "No, I don't know what you mean. Furthermore, I think that that's just a pile of shit. Do you believe it yourself?"

There was a stunned silence, but what Alinsky had done was far more useful than being polite. As one Indian described it later to some white Canadian government workers in the room, "When Mr. Alinsky told us we were full of shit, that was the first time a white man had really talked to us as equals. You would never say that to us. You would always say, 'Well, I can see your point of view but I'm a little confused,' and stuff like that. In other words you treat us as children." And the Indians decided to organize.

Alinsky's advice to organizers was to be yourselves. By being himself, and challenging others to do the same, he broke through the ritualistic ethnic games people of all cultures play with one another. He was not polite; he was not politically correct; he was just honest.

of warped acculturation, the viscerally hating, the cynically manipulating, the indifferent, the culturally jingoistic, and the paranoid.

We seldom make these distinctions and, as a result, tend to favor one recipe for all. It turns out to be no recipe, however, only words as lazy as our actions. As things stand now, America's cultures are standing on their separate turfs hurling symbols at one another. And some have divined in this the message that it is all right to hurl other things as well.

Working our way out of this jam will take a willingness to come together, to think of the future more than of the past, to learn how to enjoy our differences, and to speak honestly, without violence, of our fears and, yes, even of our prejudices. It will mean finding ways of revealing the individual under the mask of culture. It will above all take a revival of the often forgotten faith that there is a powerful advantage in doing these things. For without that, everything else we do will be a lie no matter how politely we treat each other.

> ### ELUSIVE STEREOTYPE #367
>
> A lot of liberals think of gun owners as evil, dangerous people. *Washington Post* columnist Colbert King lumped "gun junkies" in with "gay bashers"; fellow columnist William Raspberry included them with "racists" and white America firsters. That's a lot of bad people, considering that 48 percent of Americans keep guns in their homes. It also doesn't explain other gun-loving countries like Norway, Switzerland, and Canada, which are not generally known for their violent or racist ways.

Changing by being together

Janet Hampton, a George Washington University professor whose research specialty is Afro-Hispanic studies, grew up black in Kansas. She exudes a cheerful calm suggestive of having lived around a lot of love, so you might not suspect that she has taught ethnic relations to cops at the local police academy as well as been on the faculty at both mostly white and mostly black universities. Here's how she handles the first day of class: "I ask the students to tell a little about themselves. If someone is from a cultural enclave, I tell them about other students from their school or place who have really done well." She pays particular attention to those who come from "pariah nations" like Iraq. She told a student from Eritrea that he could be very helpful when the class discussed the American Civil War.

I asked her about ethnic slurs. Let's say, Jan said, that a black student used the word *wetback*. "I would make him apologize, but I would also say that we don't want to lose his point." Corrected but still valued.

Janet informs her students that "As long as you are never disrespectful, you can say anything you want . . . We will change by just being together."

Some things that help

1. **Be friendly and respectful.** In a culturally varied society it is easy to transmit signals that are misunderstood, but fortunately kindness, friendliness, and respect come across clearly. Make good use of them.
2. **Learn about other cultures.** We typically try to resolve inter-cultural tensions without giving people a solid reason for liking one another. Mutual enjoyment and admiration provide the shortest route between two ethnicities. Education is one thing that we know reduces prejudice. Yet for all our talk about diversity, this isn't so easy to come by. For example, after 4 decades of the modern civil rights movement, the University of Wisconsin is the only place in America you can get a degree in African languages and literature. We could well spend less time on abstractions of racism and more on the assets of each other's traditions.

   We could be teaching, in high school anthropology classes and college seminars, the variety of the world as something to explore and enjoy, not just as a problem or an issue. You don't have to teach diversity. Diversity is. You don't have to defend it in lofty, liberal rhetoric. Studying humanity's medley is not a moral act; it is simply intelligent. Limiting one's understanding to the "Western intellectual canon" makes as much sense as teaching bloodletting to medical students or limiting one's knowledge of the universe to data available to Copernicus. It's not that it's evil; it's just not very smart.

   And you don't have to learn it all in school. France became a haven for black exiles earlier this century in no small part because of French enthusiasm for jazz and African art. Similarly, jazz clubs and concerts were

> **TWO TIPS FROM THE REVEREND DANIEL ALDRIDGE**
>
> ✆ Don't rank things. Avoid cultural hierarchies.
> ✆ Be able to learn from other people. Admit when you don't know something.

among the few places in segregated America where apartheid was regularly ignored.

Today we are sometimes more hospitable to foreigners than we are to strangers in our own land. One notable exception is the ethnic restaurant. Why? In part because all parties involved get a fair deal out of it. In part because it is enjoyable. In part because it is natural. No one is self-conscious; no one is made to feel uncomfortable. The owner makes a good living; the customers get a good meal.

3. **Diversity within cultures counts as well as that between them.** Just because jazz is important to black culture doesn't mean all blacks like jazz. Or that colleges shouldn't recruit black cellists as well as black forwards. Or that just because someone's white, he or she has to be Anglo-Saxon or Protestant.

4. **Share power fairly.** One of the clearest manifestations of decency is equitable power. In a society wedded to winner-take-all solutions, sharing power can be difficult to achieve. But it's worth trying. One way is to learn from children. Notice how much time they spend on whether the game is "fair." They're on to something.

5. **Find something in common that's more important than what's not.** It can be a political goal, a sport, an avocation, or a business. I've seen it work in situations as diverse as a project to train church archivists or a kid's team headed for a playoff. The importance of ethnicity is often inversely proportional to what else we have on our minds.

6. **Stop being shocked by prejudice.** We have attempted to exorcise racism much as Nancy Reagan tried to get rid of drugs, by just saying no. It has worked about as well. Once we recognize the unpleasant persistence of human discrimination, once we give up the notion that it is merely social deviance controllable by sanctions, we will be guided away from puritanical corrective approaches toward ones that emphasize mitigating harm and toward activities and attitudes that become antibiotics against prejudice.

7. **Get real.** When not on the podium or in front of a mike, people in politics talk real talk about real things. Like how you're going to win the black vote or carry a Polish ward or not piss off the gays. Elsewhere, when the subject of ethnicity or sex comes up, the discussion often turns disingenuously circuitous or maddeningly abstract. This is one time when the politicians are on the right track. Lay problems and feelings honestly on the table, and then deal with them.

8. **Talk about it but not too much.** At a meeting called to discuss racial problems, a black activist said, "I don't want to talk about race unless we are going to do something specific about it." It's not a bad rule for every public discussion of race. Unproductive talk can leave people feeling more helpless and frustrated than when it began.

9. **Diversity includes people you don't like.** Even liberals don't talk about this, but a truly multicultural community will include born-again Christians opposed to abortion, Muslims with highly restrictive views on the role of women, prayer sayers and atheists, *Playboy* readers as well as Seventh-Day Adventists. Remember that you're not required to express— or even have—an opinion about everyone else in the world.

10. **Don't sweat the small stuff.** Common sense is a great civil rights tool. Even in a multicultural society, loutish sophomores are going to use tasteless language, fundamentalists will sneak in private prayers on public occasions, and eight-year-old boys will grab girls where they shouldn't. Hyperreaction to such minor phenomena hurts and trivializes the cause of human justice.

11. **Go for the important stuff.** One of the reasons the little stuff gets such big play is the lack of a clear and meaningful agenda of social justice. People wouldn't be talking so much about who said what to whom and in what tone of voice if there were a serious effort under way, for example, against discrimination in such long-neglected areas as housing and public transportation.

12. **Try to avoid putting virtues in competition.** School busing placed the virtue of integration in direct conflict with the virtue of neighborhood schools. Often we can avoid or mitigate such conflicts by choosing other tactics. For example, why was there so much attention to busing and so little to residential integration?

13. **Lighten up on the lawyers.** While of great assistance in securing basic rights, lawyers are not well equipped to deal with complex human relationships. We need to train large numbers of people who can serve as peacekeepers, mediators, and referees.

14. **Timely courage helps.** When anti-Semitic attacks began in Billings, Montana, the city responded quickly, getting rid of Nazi symbols and posting paper menorahs in the windows of homes. A little early courage at such times works better than a lot of belated hand wringing.

15. **Attack economic discrimination too.** After every group gets its rights, the powerful among it will discriminate against the weak and the

wealthy against the poor. As Saul Alinsky said, "When the poor get power, they'll be shits like everyone else." Opposition to affirmative action might have been much less had the programs been based on zip code as well as on race and sex. Martin Luther King, Jr., pointed out in 1964 that "the white poor also suffer deprivation and the humiliation of poverty if not of color. They are chained by the weight of discrimination, though its badge of degradation does not mark them. It corrupts their lives, frustrates their opportunities and withers their education."

16. **Stop worrying so much about language.** It provides a warning sign and serves as an intercultural safety valve. Paul Kuritz, in an article on ethnic humor in the *Maine Progressive,* pointed out that "as early as 1907, the English-speaking rabbis and priests of Cleveland united to protest the Irish and Jewish stage comedians. . . . The suppression of crude ethnic humor both accompanied the economic exploitation of the lower-class work force and paralleled the dismissal of the lower classes' tastes as 'offensive' to the newly refined sensibilities of upwardly-mobile second and third generation Americans."

> **ELUSIVE STEREOTYPE #383**
>
> The San Jose, California, phone book contains the name Nguyen more frequently than the name Jones.

Kuritz, a third-generation Slovak, was arguing that the real problem with a recently fired French-Canadian radio host was not that he had made fun of his own culture but that the full panoply of ethnicity was not also represented on the air. This would have allowed all these groups to experience what anthropologists call a "joking relationship," helping re-duce tensions between potentially antagonistic clans. Said Kuritz: "As a general rule of thumb, an attempt to suppress speech as 'offensive' or 'dis-empowering' is not a signal to lessen the amount of talk, but to increase the amount."

Today interethnic joking is mainly found in rough-and-tumble environ-ments, such as the modern vaudeville of comedy clubs, or in sports and politics but is frowned upon by those whose social status leads them to presume that manners create reality. The problem is that under the latter ground rules, words often disguise feelings, sidetrack action, and no longer serve to keep tension and hate apart.

17. **Be tough on leaders, not on followers.** Those with tightly defined ideas about how we should behave often make little distinction

between people who merely accept the values of their culture and those who market and manipulate them. It helps to remember that we all are creatures of our cultures and often speak with their voice. This may not be an admirable characteristic, but it certainly is a human one. After all, if it weren't for Rush, dittoheads would have nothing to ditto.

18. **Make justice pay off.** The modern civil rights movement started with a bus boycott, and many more economic actions soon followed. Its leaders understood that one of the easiest ways to get people to give up a prejudice is to discover that it's costing them money. That's why you may find more racial mixing at a shopping mall than you will in a nearby church, club, or neighborhood.

19. **Recognize that we are all part something else.** Americans have been exchanging ethnic traits for hundreds of years. Now, thanks to TV, it is virtually impossible to live in America and not have absorbed aspects of other cultures. We all, in effect, belong to a part culture, which is to say that our ethnicity is somewhat defined by its relationship to, and borrowing from, other cultures. There are almost no pure anythings in America anymore. The sooner we accept and enjoy this, the better off we'll be.

20. **Remember that everyone is an ethnic something.** There are no unethnic Americans.

Why a white guy likes living in a black city

Despite a widespread yearning for better cultural and ethnic relations, we too often only talk about problems and tensions. So let me tell you a differ-

*This information comes from my nephew, sports journalist Clemson Smith-Muniz, who does play-by-play for ESPN's Latin American broadcasts. Smith-Muniz's name would qualify as Elusive Stereotype #375 were it not for his journalistic colleague Santiago O'Connell and a Puerto Rican sportswriter named Keyvan Heydari.

ent kind of story. I offer it not as anything special but simply as an example of the sorts of things we could be telling each other but rarely do:

I'm a native Washingtonian and have lived in D.C. most of my life. D.C. is two-thirds black. When someone asks me where I live and I tell them, they sometimes look at my 50-something white face and say, "You mean *in* the city?" What they mean is: With all those blacks?

I don't live in D.C. out of any moral imperative. I'm not doing anybody except myself a favor. I live here because I enjoy it. Beside, I'd rather be in the minority in D.C. than in the majority in a lot of places. Here are a few reasons why:

- I've found black Washingtonians exceptionally friendly, decent, hospitable, and morally rooted. They're nice folks to be around.
- Black Washingtonians will talk to strangers without knowing "who are you with?" White Washingtonians, especially in the political city, are often far more formal and distant—and more likely to treat you on the basis of your utility to them. Not knowing anyone at a mostly white event in D.C. can be pretty lonely; not knowing anyone at a mostly black event in D.C. means you soon will.
- Black Washingtonians understand loss, pain, suffering, and disappointment. They have helped me become better at handling these things.
- Black Washingtonians value humor; many white Washingtonians (as Russell Baker once noted) try to be somber under the illusion that it makes them serious. I like to laugh.
- Black Washingtonians value achievement as well as power. Teachers, artists, writers, and poets are respected in the black community. As a writer I like that.
- Having other cultures nearby provides a useful gauge by which to judge one's own.
- The imagery, rhythm, and style of black speech appeal to me far more than the jargon-ridden circumlocution of the white city.
- Many black Washingtonians are actively concerned about social and political change; much of white Washington is seeking to maintain the status quo.
- White Washington always seems to want me to conform to it; black Washington has always accepted me for who I am.

Getting along with minorities of the mind

One of the hardest things for many of us is the conflict between what might be called ethnicities of the heart—the things we believe deeply, the clashing moral cultures by which we choose to live.

For example, some of the worst recent violence in this country has not involved race at all, but the issue of abortion. Attacks on abortion clinics come out of a hypertrophied sense of self-righteousness and the belief that one is entitled not only to judge but to punish those with whom you disagree.

Those favoring abortions have responded without violence, but with no less certitude, and thus many of our communities and much of our politics have become enmeshed in bitter conflict.

Worse, there are the seeds here of far more serious problems, for it is when both sides deny the existence of moral doubt that cultural values can become deadly. The slaughter in Bosnia, Rwanda, Northern Ireland, and the Middle East has not been the inevitable product of beliefs but of the unmitigated rigidity with which they are held.

Consider, for example, that three quarters of Americans believe abortion should be permitted when a woman's health is at stake, the fetus has a serious defect, or a woman has been raped. Roughly half of Americans believe an abortion should be permitted for unmarried women or mothers who don't want more children.

These figures haven't changed much in twenty years. Neither pro- nor antiabortion activists have been particularly successful in changing people's minds. We can assume that we will remain deeply divided on this issue for the foreseeable future.

> **ELUSIVE STEREOTYPE #568**
>
> Americans believe in marriage; that may be why they have so many of them. The remarriage rate of Americans is 62 percent higher than that of the Swedes, nearly 3 times that of the French, and 15 times that of the Italians. Americans give a bad marriage about two years before giving up; the Italians nine.

So what are we going to do about it? And what about a country that will continue to include both Christian fundamentalists and people who don't practice religion at all? Feminists and orthodox Muslims? Gunowners and animal rights activists? Gays, heterosexual adulterers, and people who believe in the sanctity of the male-female marriage?

Too often there is mostly the implicit notion that those who are outnumbered should shut up or go away. Periodic discussions of how many gays and lesbians there are in America, for example, seem to imply that the answer should make some policy difference. In fact, there is no minimum threshold for protection under the Constitution. The theory of that document is that even one of us counts.

> Antiabortion lecturer Dr. Jack Wilke has switched from showing grim photos of aborted fetuses to a lecture opening in which he expresses sympathy for the "agony" of the mother's decision. Said Wilke of the change: "The anger is gone, the combativeness is gone, and the questions are civil. We are listened to once again."

Being American means living in close proximity with people whose values, intrinsic nature, or behavior may be not just different, but something you may not like at all. Does that mean we should sit on our front steps and glare at our neighbors? Or worse? It doesn't have to be that way. Here are some things we all can do, regardless of what we feel in our hearts:

1. **Encourage debate, not hysteria.** Whether at a meeting, speaking to a friend, or calling a talk show, we can affect not only the substance of a debate but its tone. Keeping the discussion civil is not just a nicety; it's practical. It makes it easier to find a solution when you need one. Not only do well-run debates inform, but they take the edge off demagoguery. Besides, most people would rather be convinced than manipulated.
2. **Find ways to talk.** Even implacable foes can carry on surrogate discussions through a third party. Communities can establish cross-cultural mediation. Everyone should be encouraged to try talking before filing a lawsuit. Communities should hold regular common ground conferences at which the broadest possible spectrum of citizens—from the prominent to the pariahs—come together to find things about which they can agree.
3. **Dilute divisive issues with unifying ones.** Finding issues that bring antagonists together can help mitigate the anger they feel toward one another. A rifle-owning abortion opponent might be an important member of a committee to save the park, or a progressive might join with conservative libertarians on a ballot access issue. Remember, nothing scares politicians more than seeing people they'd rather have stay apart getting together. Besides, once you start working with these folks, you might find you actually like them.

4. **Find local solutions.** Communities are great places to find workable solutions to problems. Actually knowing people makes it much harder to see them as walking bumper stickers. Remember that behind most lawsuits and mangled public solutions to human problems were somebody's complaint—and the failure of others nearby to do something about it. Communities are where many of these problems start and where many of them could be resolved.

5. **Give each other some space.** I'm a nonchurchgoing seventh-day agnostic. My wife Kathy has taught Sunday school and has been a vestry member and church archivist. Somehow we've managed to work it out so neither of us has felt the need of a class action lawsuit to maintain our respective views of organized religion. The same could be true of most communities. But we need time and space to do our thing, play out our rituals, speak our minds, even express our annoyance and disagreement with one another.

HOW TO GET ALONG WITH OTHER AMERICANS (WHO ARE POINTING THREE GUNS AT YOUR HEAD)

Chuck Stone really knows how to get along with other Americans. Seventy-five homicide suspects surrendered personally to him, when he was columnist and senior editor of the *Philadelphia Daily News,* rather than take their chances with the Philadelphia Police Department. Black journalist Stone also negotiated the end of five hostage crises, once at gunpoint. "I learned how to listen," he says.

Stone believes in building what he calls "the reciprocity of civility." His advice for getting along with other Americans: Treat them like a member of your family.

One good rule is this: You won't have to get the judge's answer if you can work it out first. The 1st Amendment doesn't restrict free speech, but it also doesn't prohibit accommodation and compromise. Come up with a solution with which everyone's comfortable, and the ACLU never has to be the wiser.

Who's to blame?

The increase in ethnic tensions in recent years is no surprise. When an economy starts to falter, people start looking for someone to blame. The answer they often come to—with considerable help from politicians and the media—is that some other group of Americans is having all the fun.

Who's up and who's down

Why some people feel they've been screwed

Change in real hourly earnings 1979–93

1. White women college grads	Up 16%
2. Black women with two years of grad school	Up 13%
3. **All white women**	**Up 12%**
4. Black women college grads	Up 10%
5. White men with two years of grad school	Up 8%
6. **All black women**	**Up 7%**
7. White women with some college	Up 7%
8. Black women with some college	Down 1%
9. White women high school grads	Down 2%
10. White men college grads	Down 3%
11. Black men college grads	Down 3%
12. **All white men**	**Down 6%**
13. Black men with two years of grad school	Down 6%
14. Black women with high school diploma or less	Down 7%
15. **All black men**	**Down 10%**
16. White men with some college	Down 10%
17. White women with less than high school	Down 11%
18. Black men with some college	Down 16%
19. White men with high school	Down 16%
20. Black men with less than high school	Down 19%
21. Black men with high school	Down 20%
22. White men with less than high school	Down 23%

Economist Leon Keyserling once observed that when the *Titanic* sank, the men drowned and the women and children were saved. A modern sociologist looking at the statistics, he suggested, might conclude that the men died because of some particular characteristics of men. In fact, they died because there weren't enough lifeboats. This happens in the economy too.

It's easy to cite the wrong causes. In 1995 a survey found that over half of white Americans thought blacks were doing as well as or better than whites in the job market, this at a time when black unemployment was twice as high as white. The poll also showed that those who were wrong about such basic facts were twice as likely as other whites to favor cuts in food stamp spending, 50 percent more likely to oppose affirmative action, and nearly four times as likely to believe that discrimination against whites was greater than that against blacks.

On the other hand, this chart, based on data compiled by Jared Bernstein of the Economic Policy Institute, shows just how complex the issue of who is really getting what actually is. For example, white men with high school educations or less have seen a dramatic drop in earnings. Yet instead of attracting sympathy, they are often stereotyped as racists. Women seem to be doing well until you realize, for example, that women in the poorest-paying jobs earn about $100 a week less than men at the same level and that women lawyers' incomes lag behind those of males by tens of thousands of dollars. Black men are blamed for taking white jobs when in fact, they not only suffer far greater unemployment but are losing ground in wages. Black men blame black women for taking their jobs. And so forth.

What if, however we take the table above and place a piece of paper over the left-hand column so that all we see are the percentages? We now have 22 categories without any categorization. We now can see that 7 unidentified categories have done well in the period covered and that 15 have not. Stripped of our ability to expound on the role of race, sex, and education, we might recognize that there is something fundamentally wrong with such an economy. We might even find that the real problem is not race or sex but not enough jobs and not enough equity in our economic system. Then we might begin dealing with the right problem.

> My sympathies have been, and still are, strongly enlisted in behalf of that portion of them who dwell in the land which was my father's. . . . [But here in America] center all the recollections of my childhood; here are fixed all my chances at happiness, and all my hopes for my posterity.
>
> —An Irish American writing in the 1830s

So, what's next?

At least until we all become much better than we are, working things out with other Americans is going to require a lot of trial and error, a lot of patience, and a lot of forgiveness. Having a sense of humor won't hurt either.

Neither will a sense of history. We humans have come a long way from the days when we couldn't deal with anyone more foreign than our extended families or tribes. While

genocide still occurs, the world re-
gards it as an appalling remnant of
a primitive past and has organized
to prevent it—although not always
effectively. Slavery is now incon-
ceivable to most societies. Perhaps
someday obsession with race will
also be a considered a part of a cruel
past rather than an accepted way of
our relating to one another.

> I prefer to consider my subcul-
> ture, my African descent, and
> the majority culture as the yin
> and yang of my being. Different,
> the same, together, apart, one
> and not-one, utterly interdepen-
> dent, together creating some-
> thing greater than the sum of
> their parts.
> —Leonce E. Gaiter, writing in
> the *Washington Times* in the
> 1990s

Some scholars believe that the
mixture of inherited and acquired
characteristics we call race once served a useful purpose. When humans
spread throughout the world, they did not, like other creatures, need to split
genetically into new species in order to adapt to new surroundings. We
changed physically only in very limited ways. According to anthropologist
Robin Fox, man "did not have to redevelop his hairy coat in order to survive in Arctic climes; he could invent clothes." In the end our ethnic and
physical variation allowed us to live almost anywhere in the world, an astounding feat for one of the earth's creatures.

Ethnicity will not disappear. We will continue to be different from one another if for no other reason than because we come from different traditions
with different stories. And because we are rightly proud of these stories and
will try to protect them just as we protect those of our more immediate families.

At the same time, however, our notion of—and need for—race will undergo steady change. The table that follows gives a rough idea of how this
has happened in the past and how it may do so in the future. These stages of
course overlap: We watch the results of ethnic massacres in Bosnia on CNN,
then switch channels for a dose of benign ethnicity on BET or energetic,
happy multiculturalism on MTV. Some may fight against racism yet just as
strongly oppose ethnic intermarriage. Some will never lose a sense of the sa-
credness of the old ways. But increasingly race and ethnicity will be the place
we came from and not where we're going. It will remain at the core of our
experience, but it will no longer determine the limits of our dreams.

Brutal	Ethnic and racial conflict and subjugation considered normal: intense tribalism, ethnic warfare, slavery, genocide, lynching, Later modified into apartheid, segregation, and discrimination.
Benign	Formal, legal steps taken to abolish brutal racialism: desegregation, integration, affirmative action, international law against genocide, emphasis on diversity, and multiculturalism. Emphasis on legal rather than social solutions. Nationalist and ethnic backlash to many of these efforts.
Transracial	Growing acceptance of a multiracial society, though conscious ethnic divisions remain. The young lead the way. Popular arts become heavily cross-cultural; interethnic marriages increase. Intentional communities and ethnic enclaves maintain traditions to counter these trends.
Postracial	Race and ethnicity vastly decline in importance as intermarriage, cross-culturalism, and economic and social interdependence become the norm. Ethnicity remains a source of pride and tradition—our most extended family—but with far less competitive significance, less a sign of where one has come from than where one is going.

In the end how well we get along will be decided not by our cultural differences but by the significance we place upon them. We all may be creatures of our own culture, but we all are also free to determine just what that means. Most important, the future is the one culture—for better or worse—we all will inevitably share and help make. We are, each of us, brothers and sisters in the tribe of tomorrow.

12. How to find common ground
Some things we might share

We seek to be good stewards of our earth, good citizens of our country, good members of our communities, and good neighbors of those who share these places with us.

We reject the immoderate tone of current politics, its appeal to hate and fear, its scorn for democracy, its preference for conflict over resolution, its servility to money and to those who possess it, and its deep indifference to the problems of ordinary Americans.

We seek a cooperative commonwealth based on decency before profit, liberty before sterile order, justice before efficiency, happiness before uniformity, families before systems, communities before corporations, and people before institutions.

We believe we should treat our politics, our country, and one another with common decency, common sense, and a search for common ground.

When issues divide us deeply, we should seek ways to discuss them both honestly and with reason, out of the glare of the media and away from others who profit from our divisions.

We should tread gently upon the earth and leave it in better condition than we found it.

The physical and cultural variety of human beings is a gift and not a threat. We are glad that the world includes many who are different from ourselves by nature, principle, inclination, or faith.

We must protect the right of others to disagree with us so we shall be free to speak our own minds.

Our national economic goal is the self-sufficiency, well-being, and stability of our communities and those living in them.

Ecological principles should determine economic policies and not vice versa.

The first source of expertise is the wisdom of the people.

Individuals possess fundamental rights that are inalienable and not contingent on responsibilities assigned by the state. These rights are to be restrained only by a due concern for the health, safety, and liberty of others and are not to be made subservient to the arbitrary and capricious dictates of the government.

Citizens should participate as directly as possible in our democracy.

The media should inform citizens and provide a means by which citizens may address government rather than serve as a vehicle by which members of the government and elites tell citizens what to think.

Power should be devolved to the lowest practical level.

The Bill of Rights and other constitutional provisions have deep permanence and are not to be manipulated or abridged for political gain.

Politics dependent on corporate financing and lobbyist influence is corrupt, antidemocratic, and unacceptable.

Simplicity, conservation, and recycling should be central to our economy, our politics, and our lives.

Individual privacy is paramount and not to be subservient to the needs of the state.

Individual rights are manifestly superior to any rights granted to corporations.

Our elected officials are servants and representatives, not rulers.

We need more community more than we need more things.

We are citizens and not merely taxpayers.

We own our government and are not merely its consumers.

13. How to do something about it

Getting started.
Good repair shops,
ideal mills, and stuff to read

Communities

CO-HOUSING

EcoVillage
Annabel Taylor Hall
Cornell University
Ithaca, NY 14853
607-255-8276 Fax: 607-255-9985
ecovillage@cornell.edu
http://www.cfe.cornell.edu/
ecovillage/evi.html
A major environmentally focused
cohousing community.

SOCIAL INDICATORS

Sustainable Seattle
Metrocenter YMCA
909 Fourth Ave.
Seattle, WA 98104
206-382-5013 x5072
sustea@halcyon.com
http://www.scn.org/sustainable/
susthome.html
A leader in community-based social
indicators.

MEDIA

The Neighborhood Works
Center for Neighborhood
Technology
2125 West North Ave.
Chicago, IL 60647
312-278-4800 Fax: 312-278-3840
tnwedit@cnt.org
http://www.cnt.org/tnw/
This publication is full of news of use to
community organizations.

Urban Ecologist
Urban Ecology
405 14th St. #900
Oakland, CA 94612
510-251-6330 Fax: 510-251-2117
urbanecology@igc.apc.org
http://www.best.com/
~schmitty/uejournal.shtml
A constant source of ideas for better
urban life.

PUBLIC MARKETS

Project for Public Spaces
153 Waverly Place
New York, NY 10014
212-620-5660 Fax: 212-620-3821
pps@pps.org
http://www.pps.org
A nonprofit planning and design organization working to create more enjoyable, comfortable, and economically useful public spaces.

BOOKS

Building Cities That Work by Edmund D. Fowler. An excellent look at the post–World War II city and its discontent. Especially useful in its comments on crime and about children. *McGill-Queen's University Press, Montreal, 1993.*

The Careless Society: Community and Its Counterfeits by John McKnight. A good introduction to the ideas of one of professionalism's most cogent critics and community's most articulate supporters. *Basic Books, New York, 1995.*

City Comforts: How to Build an Urban Village by David Sucher. Proving that good planning is in the details, Sucher offers a long list of suggestions (with photos) on how to improve urban life, including how to squeeze a corner store into a parking garage and how to make life easier for bicyclists. *City Comforts Press, Seattle, 1995.*

Cities and the Wealth of Nations by Jane Jacobs. An important analysis of the economics of cities. *Random House, New York, 1991.*

The Death and Life of Great American Cities by Jane Jacobs. Jacobs's classic work. *Vintage Books, New York, 1961.*

Democracy

American Civil Liberties Union
132 West 43d St.
New York, NY 10036
212-944-9800
info@aclu.org
faq@ACLU.org
http://www.aclu.org
It may make you mad from time to time, but few organizations have done as much to keep America a democracy as the ACLU.

Ecology

BOOKS

Environment in Peril, edited by Anthony B. Wolbarst. The hard copy product of talks to Environmental Protection Agency staff by some of the world's leading ecological thinkers. Excellent summary of current environmental issues. *Smithsonian Press, Washington, D. C., 1991.*

For the Common Good: Redirecting the Economy toward Community, the Enviroment and a Sustainable Future by Herman E. Daley and John B. Cobb, Jr. The ecological alternatives to corporate globalism. *Beacon Press, Boston 1989.*

The Population Explosion by Paul and Anne Ehrlich. The relationship between population growth and the environment. *Simon and Schuster, New York, 1990*

State of the World and **Vital Signs** by the Worldwatch Institute. Great reference material on the state of the global environment. *W.W. Norton, New York, annual.*

Economics

COOPERATIVES

Co-Op America
1612 K St. NW #600
Washington, DC 20006
202-872-5307 Fax: 202-331-8166
A clearinghouse of information on
cooperatives.

National Cooperative
Business Association
1401 New York Ave. NW #1100
Washington, DC 20005
202-638-6222 Fax: 202-638-1374
ncba@ncbc.org

COMMUNITY CURRENCY

E. F. Schumacher Society
140 Jug End Rd.
Great Barrington, MA 02130
413-528-1737 Fax: 413-528-4472
efssociety@aol.com
http://members.aol.com/efssociety
Good source of information on the
history and development of community
currency.

Ithaca Money
Box 6578
Ithaca, NY 14851
ithacahour@aol.com
Offers a local currency kit, including
forms, laws, procedures, and samples.

Time Dollar Network
5500 39th St. NW
Washington, DC 20015
202-686-5200 Fax: 202-537-5033
timedollar@aol.com
http://www.cfg.com/timedollar
Clearinghouse on how to use service
credits and time dollars.

CORPORATIONS

Program on Corporations,
Law & Democracy
POB 806
Cambridge, MA 02140
508-487-3151 Fax: 508-487-3151
Excellent material on the history of
corporate power and what can be done
about it.

CREDIT UNIONS

Community Credit Union Services
1722 Seventh St NW
Washington, DC 20001
202-328-9805

National Federation of Community
Development Credit Unions
120 Wall Street (10th floor)
New York, NY 10005-3902
212-809-1850 Fax: 212-809-3274
nfcdcu@nyc.pipeline.com
http://www.natfed.org

DEBT REFORM

Sovereignty
1154 West Logan St.
Freeport, IL 61032
815-232-8737 Fax: 815-232-5313
sovgntyken@aol.com
A movement to encourage the issuance
of interest-free federal loans to state
and localities for public works projects
and for the reduction of debt.

EMPLOYEE OWNERSHIP

National Center
for Employee Ownership
1201 Martin Luther King Ave.
Oakland, CA 94612
510-272-9461 Fax: 510-272-7510
nceo@nceo.org
http://www.nceo.org
Information and membership
organization for people interested in
employee ownership.

ECONOMIC INDICATORS

Redefining Progress
1 Kearny St. (4th floor)
San Francisco, CA 94108
415-781-1191 Fax: 415-781-1198
info@rprogress.org
This group is developing the genuine progress indicator as an alternative to the gross domestic product. Offers publications and other materials.

MEDIA

Left Business Observer
250 W. 85th St.
New York, NY 10024-3217
212-874-4020 Fax: 212-874-3137
dhenwood@panix.com
http://www.panix.com/~dhenwood/
LBO__home.html
Perceptive critic of conventional economics and the bad politics that result from it.

SHORTER WORK TIME

Shorter Work-Time Group
POB 44-1615
West Somerville, MA 02144-0013
617-628-5558
Working to build coalitions around shorter worktime issues

BOOKS

The End of Work by Jeremy Rifkin. *Putnam's, New York, 1995.*

New Money for Healthy Communities by Tom Greco. Good summary of local currencies. *Box 42663, Tucson, AZ 85733.*

Nonfinancial Economics by Eugene J. McCarthy and William McGaughey, *Praeger, New York, 1989.*

The Overworked American by Juliet B. Schor, *Basic Books, New York, 1991.*

Time Dollars by Edgar Cahn and Jonathan Rowe. Using the homegrown currency of time to rebuild the nonmarket economy of neighborliness and community. *Rodale, Emmaus, PA, 1992. (Out of print, but available from Time Dollars Network, 202-686-5200)*

Whole Life Economics: Revaluing Daily Life by Barbara Brandt. *New Society, Philadelphia, 1995.*

Justice

ALTERNATIVE JUSTICE

National Center
on Institutions & Alternatives
635 Slaters Lane #G100
Alexandria, VA 22314
703-684-0373 Fax: 703-684-6037
ncia@igc.apc.org
http://www.ncianet.org/ncia
National authority on justice issues. Provides research and services on prisons, community-based sanctions, rehabilitation, cost comparison, crime prevention, treatment of sex offenders, racial disparity, drug offenses, jail suicides, and more.

DISPUTE SETTLEMENT

National Association
for Mediation in Education
1726 M St. NW #500
Washington, DC 20036-4502
202-466-4764 Fax: 202-466-4769
nidr@igc.apc.org
Association for conflict resolution in education

National Association
for Community Mediation
1726 M St. NW #500
Washington, DC 20036-4502
202-467-6226 Fax: 202-466-4769
nafcm@igc.apc.org

DRUGS

Drug Policy Foundation
4455 Connecticut Ave. NW #B-500
Washington, DC 20008
202-537-5005 Fax: 202-537-3007
dpf@dpf.org
The organization leading the fight against drug prohibition.

National Organization for the Reform of Marijuana Laws
1001 Connecticut Ave. NW #1010
Washington, DC 20036
202-483-5500 Fax: 202-483-0057
naplnorml@aol.com
http://www.norml.org
NORML is fighting for repeal of repressive and ineffective laws against marijuana.

JURY RIGHTS

Fully Informed Jury Association
POB 59
Helmville, MT 59843
406-793-5550
Organizing efforts to require that juries be told of their right to judge both the law and the facts.

BOOKS

Above the Law: Secret Deals, Political Fixes, and Other Misadventures of the US Department of Justice by David Burnham. The most comprehensive look at how the prosecution of federal crimes is really carried out. *Scribner, New York, 1996.*

America's Longest War: Rethinking Our Tragic Crusade against Drugs by Steven B. Duke and Albert C. Gross. The history of America's wars against drugs, their social and economic costs, and various alternatives. *Tarcher, Los Angeles, 1994.*

Safe Cities: Guidelines for Planning, Design and Management by Gerda R. Wekerle and Carolyn Whitzman. In straightforward and well-illustrated fashion, this book explains how our places can be made safer. *Van Nostrand Reinhold, New York, 1995.*

Smoke and Mirrors: The War on Drugs and the Politics of Failure by Dan Baum. The story of our failed current antidrug policy and how it came about. *Little, Brown, Boston, 1996.*

We the Jury: The Jury System and the Ideal of Democracy by Jeffrey Abrahamson. An excellent review of juries and their important role in democracy. *Basic Books, New York, 1994.*

Media

INTERNET

Electronic Privacy Information Center
666 Pennsylvania Ave. #301
Washington, DC 20003
202-544-9240 Fax: 202-547-5482
info@epic.org
http://www.epic.org
A sort of ACLU of the Internet. Has been effective at organizing opposition to Net censorship.

MEDIA WATCHDOGS

FAIR
130 W. 25th St.
New York, NY 10001
212-633-6700 Fax: 212-727-7668
fair@fair.org
http://www.iqc.apc.org/fair
FAIR is a liberal media watchdog group. Publishes an informative newsletter, *Extra!*

PUBLIC RELATIONS

20/20 Vision
1828 Jefferson Place NW
Washington, DC 20036
202-833-2020 Fax: 202-833-5307
vision@igc.apc.org
http://www.2020vision.org
Good guides to dealing with the media
and the bureaucracy

SALONS

National Salon Association
Utne Reader
1624 Harmon Place #330
Minneapolis, MN 55403
612-338-5040 Fax: 612-638-6043
salons@utne.com
http://www.utne.com
Where you can find out about any of
250 neighborhood salons operating all
over North America

STUDY CIRCLES

Study Circles Resource Center
POB 203
Pomfret, CT 06258
860-928-2616 Fax: 860-928-3713
scrc@neca.com
How to organize a study circle, sample
programs, bibliography.

Politics

BALLOT ACCESS

Ballot Access
Box 470296
San Francisco, CA 94147
415-922-9779 Fax: 415-441-4268
ban@igc.apc.org
http://www.well.com/conf/liberty/
ban/index.html
Informative newsletter on third-party
and ballot access issues.

CAMPAIGN FINANCE

Center for Responsive Politics
1320 19th St. NW #700
Washington, DC 20036
202-857-0044 Fax 202-857-7809
info@crp.org
http://www.crp.org
Whatever your solution to campaign
financing, CRP is an invaluable research
resource for both activists and
journalists. Particularly good
publications.

Working Group
on Electoral Democracy
70 Washington St.
Brattleboro, VT 05301
Working toward full public financing of
political campaigns.

ELECTION REFORM

Center for Voting and Democracy
POB 60037
Washington, DC 20039
202-828-3062
cvd@essential.org
http://www.igc.apc.org/cvd/
Leading the way to proportional
representation, preference voting, and
other fairer systems of counting ballots
than the one we use now. Sells
software to communities and
organizations for use in carrying out
preference voting.

NEW POLITICS

Listed below are a few of the
organizations pressing for a new
politics in this country. Those most in
accord with the ideas expressed in this
book are noted with a check.

☑**Association of State Green Parties**
2244 Lindsay Lot Rd.
Shippensburg, PA 17257
(717) 530-0931
ss4538@ark.ship.edu
www.greenparties.org
With ballot status in an increasing
number of states, the Green Party is the
leading progressive alternative to the
two traditional parties. This association
is the link to state and local Green
parties around the country.

☑**Alliance for Democracy**
P.O. Box 683
Lincoln, MA 01773-0683
617-259-9395 Fax: 617-259-0404
peoplesall@aol.com
http://www.igc.apc.org/alliance
A new populist alliance attempting to
revive the politics and the spirit of the
traditional populist movement.
Chapters are sprouting up all over the
country

New Party
227 W. 40th St. #1303
New York, NY 10018
212-302-5053 Fax: 212-302-5344
newparty@newparty.org
http://www.newparty.org
Runs progressive candidates in
independent and nonpartisan contests
but avoids direct competition with
Democrats.

Libertarian Party
2600 Virginia Ave. NW #100
Washington, DC 20037
202-333-0008 Fax: 202-333-0072
lphq@digex.com
http://www.lp.org/lp/
Excellent on civil liberties issues, such as
those involving abortion, drugs, gays,
etc. However, Libertarians also oppose
restrictions on property rights and want
only minimal government.

POLITICAL RESEARCH

Project Vote Smart
129 NW Fourth St. #204
Corvallis, OR 97330
800-622-SMART Fax: 541-754-2747
comments@vote-smart.org
http://www.vote-smart.org
An invaluable source of information on
politics and government, including
voting records of politicians. Research
assistance is available.

TELEDEMOCRACY

Teledemocracy Network
c/o Ted Becker
Dept. of Political Science
Room 7080, Haley Center
Auburn University, AL 36845
334-844-6161 Fax: 334-844-5348
becketl@mail.auburn.edu
http://www.auburn.edu/tann
Electronic and mail voting, electronic
town meetings, and the like are all
meat for this group promoting
cyberdemocracy. Informative Web site.

TOWN MEETINGS

Citizens Guide on Town Meeting by
Kenneth Bresler. 16-page booklet on
how town meetings work in
Massachusetts. Ordering information:
*State Bookstore, State House, Room
116, Boston MA, 02133. 617-727-2834.*

Other good things

BOOKS

The Use of Lateral Thinking by
Edward De Bono. One of De Bono's
guides to practical thinking, and a good
place to start. *Penguin Books, New
York, 1967.* Another is **De Bono's
Thinking Course,** which also covers
such topics as thinking/doing and
perceptions/patterns. *Facts on File, New
York, 1994.*

Where We Stand by Michael Wolff, et al. Prepared for a PBS series. Contains more than 1,000 rankings of countries in categories ranging from sex practices to recycling. It's a few years old but still an excellent guide comparing America with the rest of the world. *Bantam Books, New York, 1992.*

A People's History of the United States by Howard Zinn. A great source for everything you didn't learn about U.S. history in high school and college. *Harper Perennial, New York, 1990.*

GROUPS

E. F. Schumacher Society
140 Jug End Rd.
Great Barrington, MA 02130
413-528-1737 fax: 413-528-4472
efssociety@aol.com
http://members.aol.com/efssociety
Library literature and programs for those who know that small is beautiful.

PUBLICATIONS

The Progressive Review
1739 Connecticut Ave. NW
Washington, DC 20009
202-232-5544 Fax: 202-234-6222
ssmith@igc.apc.org
http://emporium.turnpike.net/P/
ProRev/index.htm
Where the author hangs out.

Utne Reader
1624 Harmon Place
Minneapolis, MN 55403
612-338-5040 Fax: 612-638-6043
info@utne.com
http://www.utne.com
The essential digest of alternative America

Yes!: A Journal of Positive Futures
POB 10818
Bainbridge Island, WA 98110
206-842-0216 Fax: 206-842-5208
yes@futurenet.org
http://www.futurenet.org
Important reading about social and economic alternatives that is often years ahead of the conventional media.

Never doubt that a small group of thoughtful, committed people can change the world. Indeed it is the only thing that has.

—Margaret Mead

This all happened
with a little help
from my friends

Anne Depue
Kara Milner
Alane Mason
Tom Martin
Rob Richie
Jon Rowe
Kathy Smith
Eric Sterling
Tony Wolbarst

Parts of this book appeared in different form
in the *Progressive Review* and the *Utne Reader*